The TRULY HEALTHY *Vegetarian* COOKBOOK

Hearty Plant-Based Recipes for Every Type of Eater

ELIZABETH THOMSON

Photography by Hélène Dujardin

ROCKRIDGE PRESS

Design by Nami Kurita

Photography © Helene Dujardin, 2018; styling by Tami Hardeman

ISBN: Print 978-1-64152-021-8 | eBook 978-1-64152-022-5

THE TRULY HEALTHY
VEGETARIAN COOKBOOK

To my wonderful husband, Alex, who washes endless piles of dishes and encourages me to chase all of my crazy dreams.

CONTENTS

CHAPTER 5

Substantial Salads 55

CHAPTER 6

Soups and Stews 75

CHAPTER 7

Wraps, Sandwiches, and Burgers 89

FOREWORD

When Liz told me she was in the process of writing a cookbook, I was confident that her book would be a valuable resource for both vegetarians and omnivores. And indeed, this cookbook is full of both nourishing plant-based recipes and tools and tips to make the vegetarian lifestyle more approachable for everyone. I have known Liz virtually via the food blogging world for a long time, and have always admired her dedication to making real, plant-based meals simple and exciting. *The Truly Healthy Vegetarian Cookbook* is an extended reflection of her passion for the vegetarian lifestyle.

Plant-based eating has long been known to be beneficial for both health and environmental reasons. Recently, however, it has gained an extraordinary momentum that's very exciting to me as a registered dietitian. Thanks to a combination of support from renowned personalities, the hard work of educators, and demand from the public, plant-based eating is slowly transitioning from fringe to mainstream. It is a breath of fresh air to see more people experimenting with vegetarian cooking, and there is no better time than now to embark on the journey.

In *The Truly Healthy Vegetarian Cookbook*, Liz gives guidance on how to approach vegetarianism in a healthier manner. A healthy vegetarian lifestyle promotes fewer processed and refined foods and more unprocessed plant-based meals. In her book, Liz demystifies these ingredients and cooking techniques. From delectable Oven-Roasted Portobello Fajitas (page 107) to Vegan Black Bean Brownie Bites (page 147), Liz brings together the very best of vegetable-centric dishes in a way everyone can easily replicate in their own kitchens.

In addition to her recipes, this book will be instrumental in providing insights into the basics of a vegetarian diet, with tips and tricks to help avoid the pitfalls of unhealthy vegetarian eating, and inspiration to make meatless meals regularly. I sincerely hope *The Truly Healthy Vegetarian Cookbook* will find its way into everyone's kitchen as an inspiration for vegetable enthusiasts, novice vegetarians, and home cooks everywhere.

Dixya Bhattarai, MS, RD, LD
Registered Dietitian Nutritionist
Blogger at *Food, Pleasure, and Health*

INTRODUCTION

T ruffle macaroni and cheese, a tower of nachos, or my personal favorite, deep-dish pizza—all are vegetarian. *Vegetarian food* is no longer synonymous with *salad*. But while there are lots of delicious dishes that full-time, part-time, or Meatless Monday vegetarians can enjoy, that doesn't mean those dishes are healthy. Welcome to *The Truly Healthy Vegetarian Cookbook*, where you will find more than 100 recipes that are hearty, satisfying, and healthy, too. Those are not mutually exclusive—I promise!

Growing up in the Midwest during the 1990s, I didn't know what kale was. I'd never seen a sweet potato that wasn't topped with marshmallows. Ranch dressing was a standard pizza topping, and my favorite thing to order at a restaurant was french fries. When I was in college, I decided to become a vegetarian. I thought I was being healthy by replacing meat with boxes of crackers, burritos filled with white rice, heaps of macaroni and cheese, and of course, plenty of pizza. While there's a time and place for these foods, eating this way every day wasn't what my body needed to stay energized.

I counted calories, but I didn't think about the actual ingredients of the foods I was eating. I didn't really know how to cook, so I relied on frozen meals and convenience foods. After a while, though, I started reading labels. That's when I decided tearing open a box of pasta and topping it with a mysterious powdery sauce wasn't doing me any favors, and I started focusing on the ingredients I was putting into my body. When I did, I realized that whole foods were a much more nutritious option. It didn't mean I had to give up all my favorite meals; I just started making little swaps so I could enjoy my favorite dishes in a healthier way.

In 2010, I started a food blog as a way to teach myself how to cook. I wanted to ditch the "100-calorie pack" way of eating and learn how to prepare healthy meals with whole-food ingredients. It felt like a challenge at first, because there were so many ingredients I was unfamiliar with, and following a complicated recipe was intimidating. But once I got started in the kitchen, I couldn't stop. I fell in love with creating recipes and transforming simple ingredients into easy, healthy dishes that really satisfied me. I've learned plenty of tips and tricks since then to make cooking healthy food part of my daily routine, and I'm excited to share some of my favorite time-saving, budget-friendly, and flavor-boosting tips with you. When people ask me if it's hard to be a vegetarian, I tell them that I honestly can't remember life any other way!

When I first met my husband, he was a meat eater who wanted to start eating a more plant-based diet. After a few months of dating, he quickly learned that eating vegetarian isn't difficult or complicated. He gets the health benefits that come along with a vegetarian diet but still enjoys a few of his favorite meat dishes now and then. Even if you're not ready to give up meat entirely (or if some people in your family are vegetarian and others aren't), you can still enjoy the health perks of these vegetarian recipes.

All of the recipes in this book are dishes I love to make in my own kitchen. Whether it's a Friday-night dinner party with friends or a busy Tuesday night with kids, I hope these recipes will become favorites in your house.

CHAPTER 1

Healthy and Satisfied

Healthy eating can often seem difficult, expensive, or complicated, but it doesn't have to be. In this chapter, I'll talk about how plant-based foods fuel your body and share the pantry staples that will help these meals come together easily. You don't have to make dramatic changes to your lifestyle right away—just take a step toward more plant-based foods and your body will thank you!

I've been a vegetarian for more than 10 years, but it didn't happen overnight. I slowly phased out meat in high school, but it wasn't until college that I officially decided to go vegetarian. When I started, I didn't understand how to replace meat with truly healthy options. I enjoyed some vegetables, but I ate almost nothing except carbohydrates. While there is nothing wrong with healthy carbs, I was picky and didn't like trying new foods, which meant I ate a lot of pasta and bagels with peanut butter.

Eventually, I learned that health was about more than just counting calories and that the ingredients I put into my body had a direct impact on how I felt. When I started incorporating more whole, plant-based foods into my diet, I noticed I had more energy. My skin was clearer. I didn't feel hungry all the time. And I stopped worrying about calories.

Why Ditch Meat?

Whether you're already a vegetarian or you're just thinking about eating a little less meat, I hope this book will be a great resource for you. I'm the only one in my family who is 100 percent vegetarian, but over the years, the rest of my family has started eating more plant-based foods. The good news (for them and you) is that you don't have to be a strict vegetarian to enjoy some of the benefits of a plant-based diet.

FOR YOUR HEALTH

Focusing on whole, plant-based foods isn't just good for your waistline. Plant-based foods are good for your whole body, literally from your head to your toes. Studies have shown that vegetarians have a lower risk of high blood pressure and type 2 diabetes. Vegetarians typically have an easier time getting the recommended servings of fruits and vegetables because their meals can be centered on plants. Even if you're not ready to give up meat entirely, your body can still benefit simply by replacing some of the meat you eat with plant-based foods.

People who eat a vegetarian diet also tend to have a lower BMI (body mass index, a measure of body fat based on height and weight) and lower rates of obesity. This could be attributed to a number of things, but one simple reason is that fruits and vegetables aren't very calorie dense. If you've ever struggled with portion control, vegetables are an easy way to fill up. Of course, simply eating a vegetarian diet isn't necessarily a cure-all, and there are plenty of not-so-healthy vegetarian foods, but as you learn to incorporate healthy, plant-based foods into your diet, your body will reap the benefits.

FOR YOUR WALLET

There's a misconception that healthy eating has to be expensive, but it can actually be a cost-effective way to eat. A plant-based diet has been shown to be quite a bit cheaper than a diet that includes animal protein. Plant-based proteins, like lentils and beans, are inexpensive protein sources, so cutting back on meat can significantly lower your grocery bill. For example, ground beef, a relatively inexpensive meat, is typically between $3 and $4 a pound. If you were to purchase organic, grass-fed ground beef, it might be closer to $6 to $7 a pound. In contrast, a pound of lentils costs less than $2, and that would be enough lentils to feed a family of four! While fresh produce can occasionally be pricey, there are delicious frozen produce options that can be just as tasty, for a fraction of the cost.

Eating a vegetarian diet also has a positive effect on the environment. Producing 1 pound of animal protein uses 12 times more land, 13 times more fossil fuel, and 15 times more water than producing 1 pound of plant-based protein. In fact, a 2006 report from the United Nations found that raising animals for food generates more greenhouse gases than all the cars and trucks in the world combined. Whether it's for your own health or the health of the planet, eating less meat can have a positive effect on your life.

Meatless Does Not Equal Healthy

There are tons of packaged and processed vegetarian foods that will try to fool you into thinking they're healthy because they're meatless. Similarly, just because a food is organic or expensive doesn't mean it's good for you. Oftentimes, meat is replaced by a refined carbohydrate or a dairy product. While these foods are meatless, they might not be healthy. In fact, it can be easy to fall into the trap of a high-carb, high-sugar diet when you're eating vegetarian.

AN UNHEALTHY VEGETARIAN DIET

Pizza is vegetarian. Cookies are vegetarian. Macaroni and cheese is vegetarian. All of these delicious foods have a place (so don't worry, I'm not asking you to give them up!), but be aware that a vegetarian diet isn't a shortcut to health. You still have to make healthy choices.

A typical vegetarian diet could be a bowl of cereal for breakfast, pasta for lunch, crackers and cheese for a snack, and pizza for dinner. That's already carb heavy, but you might not notice that your cereal is loaded with added sugar or that your lunch is full of refined carbohydrates that won't keep you energized throughout the afternoon. If you've ever felt that 2 p.m. sugar crash, you know the downside of eating a high-sugar/refined-carb diet that lacks substance. If you're not focusing on whole foods, protein, fiber, and complex carbohydrates, your body will end up feeling tired and hungry.

It's important to choose foods that fill you up and keep you full. When you're deciding what to eat, aim for a balance of complex carbohydrates (the kind that come from whole grains and vegetables), fiber, protein, and fat. Speaking of fat, don't shy away from it—just try to focus on plant-based sources of fat, which are much healthier.

It's no surprise that there are many definitions of *healthy*. I like to think of *healthy* as a balanced approach to food and nutrition. There's a time and a place for kale and a time and a place for a cupcake. Since I'm guessing you don't need any help eating cupcakes, this book will focus on healthy recipes featuring whole ingredients and proper portions.

I'll talk about the benefits of complex carbohydrates and how to ensure that you're eating a good balance of carbohydrates, fat, and protein. The recipes will use healthy, plant-based sources of fat, and each will fill you up with protein and fiber to keep you satisfied. I'll give you plenty of tips and tricks along the way to help with preparation, substitutions, and nutrition, but let's start with four basic guidelines for a healthy diet.

STEP 1. CHOOSE WHOLE FOODS

The recipes in this book focus primarily on whole foods. They don't contain things like artificial sweeteners or fake meat. You'll see lots of vegetables and legumes, such as black beans and lentils; nuts and seeds, like almonds and chia seeds; and some healthy carbs, like 100 percent whole-wheat flour.

I'll also teach you how to swap out some of your favorite ingredients for more nutritious (but still delicious) whole-food options. For example, you can trade regular pasta for whole-wheat pasta or vegetable noodles. Where you might normally use mayonnaise, try avocado. Eventually, you might find yourself skipping bottled salad dressing, which is often loaded with heavily processed oils and sugars, and reaching for a salad dressing you made yourself.

Types of Vegetarian Diet

There are a few different types of vegetarian diet; they stem from different health preferences and belief systems. Whether you're a strict vegetarian or you're just trying to eat less meat, all of the recipes in this book are lacto-ovo-vegetarian-friendly, with options for substitutions based on your preferences.

Lacto-ovo-vegetarians eat eggs and dairy products but not meat.

Lacto-vegetarians eat dairy products but not eggs or meat.

Ovo-vegetarians eat eggs but not dairy products or meat.

Vegans do not eat meat, dairy products, eggs, or any other products (such as honey) derived from animals.

There might be a few ingredients in the book that sound unfamiliar, such as tempeh or nutritional yeast. (For the record, nutritional yeast is just deactivated yeast. It has a cheesy, nutty flavor that can be a great substitute if you're avoiding dairy. It's also a great source of protein.) Don't worry, though—most of these recipes will use ingredients that you probably already have in your kitchen.

STEP 2. MEAL PLANNING AND PREP

Meal planning doesn't have to be complicated or time-consuming. Thinking ahead about what meals you plan to make for the week can help you eat a healthier diet, save money at the grocery store, and avoid a last-minute trip to the market for one ingredient. Even if you're shooting for just one or two vegetarian meals each week, a little bit of planning can make a big difference.

Prepping a few meals, or even just a few steps, ahead of time can keep you on track. Takeout is less tempting when you already have dinner in the refrigerator. But don't worry, I'm not going to ask you to spend your entire Sunday cooking lentils. Just a few shortcuts can help you speed through the process. Here are a few of my favorite meal prep tips:

- Make a big batch of quinoa in a rice cooker, or on the stove top if you don't have a rice cooker. Quinoa can be used just like rice in lots of recipes. Cooking a batch ahead of time makes it easy to add a scoop to soups, stews, salads, and wraps.

- Wash and chop things like celery and carrots as soon as you get home from the grocery store. These vegetables are often used as a base for soups and sauces, and they keep well in an airtight container in the refrigerator for 7 to 10 days.

- Rather than buying precut fruits and vegetables, which can be quite expensive, consider purchasing frozen produce, which tends to be cheaper. Frozen vegetables are delicious in soups and stir-frys and don't require any washing or chopping. Frozen fruits can easily be tossed into a smoothie or yogurt bowl with no extra prep work.

- Roast a big batch of vegetables all at once. Sweet potatoes, broccoli, and green beans are particularly great choices to roast ahead of time. I love sprinkling roasted vegetables with salt and pepper and tossing them into my favorite salads, but they can also be easily added to wraps, tacos, and sandwiches.

- Don't buy foods you won't use. That might sound obvious, but a lot of people waste money on foods they think they should eat, even though they don't like them. If you hate broccoli, don't load up your cart with broccoli. Pick a green vegetable that you'll actually want to eat. Food that goes bad in your crisper drawer won't do you any good.

STEP 3. BALANCE YOUR PLATE

You'll notice that in this cookbook, the recipes include a balance of carbohydrates, protein, and fat. The balance of nutrients is important, because while the carbs give you energy, the protein and fat can help you feel satisfied and full. Don't skimp on the healthy fats from things like avocados and olive oil. These are important components in helping your body feel full and satisfied.

Since vegetarian recipes don't usually have a main source of protein, it can be hard to brainstorm new ideas for dinner. This book will help you rethink your plate and give you new ideas for healthy, satisfying meals. New dishes can be particularly hard for kids, especially if ingredients look unfamiliar. When introducing a new ingredient, whether it's Brussels sprouts or hummus, sometimes it can help to serve it with something familiar. For example, instead of serving hummus with an unfamiliar vegetable, pair it with baby carrots or cucumbers.

STEP 4. EAT SENSIBLE PORTIONS

Don't forget the importance of proper portions. Even healthy foods aren't so healthy if you're eating too much. All of the recipes here have moderate portion sizes. For some people, it might be easier to eat smaller meals with more snacks in between. Others might prefer three larger meals.

However you prefer to break it up, make sure you're not eating until you're completely stuffed. Pay attention to your hunger cues, and eat slowly so your body has a chance to let you know when it's had enough. Many of these recipes contain "high-volume" foods, which means you can still have a substantial portion without overeating. For example, I love piling up pasta dishes with fresh vegetables because it means I can have a larger portion without going crazy on calories or carbohydrates.

The Nutritious Vegetarian Kitchen

Once you stock your kitchen with a few essential ingredients, you'll be on your way to a nutritious vegetarian lifestyle. Below, I share some of my favorite protein sources, healthy fats, and complex carbs. With this core list of ingredients, it's easy to mix and match your way to healthy cooking.

POWER PROTEINS

"But where do you get your protein?" I've been asked this typical question for years and years, and people are often surprised when I rattle off a long list of foods. Most people don't realize that 1 cup of Greek yogurt contains 17 grams of protein, 1 cup of cooked wild

Super Satisfiers

Here are some great ingredients to add to meals if you're particularly hungry.

Quinoa: Whether it's tossed into a salad or mixed into soup, quinoa is an excellent source of protein. And since it has a neutral flavor, it's easy to add to just about any meal.

Nuts and seeds: A handful of sunflower seeds, almonds, or walnuts is a heart-healthy snack. You can also sprinkle them on top of oatmeal and salads, and even in sandwiches.

Nut butters: Peanut butter and almond butter are great bases for stir-fry sauces and salad dressings. Try them swirled into yogurt and smoothies or as a dip with fruit.

Plain Greek yogurt: Yogurt isn't just for breakfast! It's a perfect sour cream swap on top of tacos or chili. It's also a great way to add a little extra protein to your meal.

Avocado: Is there anything avocado can't do? It can be blended into a smoothie, added to salads, spread onto a sandwich, or sliced onto tacos and casseroles.

Chickpeas: Roasted chickpeas are one of my favorite quick and easy snacks. Try tossing them on top of a salad or in a wrap. Whether you like them spicy, salty, or savory, they're a tasty and versatile ingredient.

rice contains 6 grams of protein, 2 tablespoons of peanut butter contain 8 grams, and even kale has 3 grams of protein per cup! There are plenty of plant-based ways to get enough protein.

Here are my top 10 power proteins that I love to incorporate into meals.

1. Tempeh: Tempeh is made of fermented soybeans, and it's actually less processed than tofu. I love the hearty texture, and a 3-ounce serving contains 16 grams of protein and just 140 calories.

2. Lentils: Lentils contain 9 grams of protein per ½-cup serving. A bowl of lentil soup can easily provide more than 30 grams of protein.

3. Chickpeas: Not only are chickpeas a super versatile ingredient, but they also contain 6 grams of protein per ½-cup serving.

4. Edamame: Whether you enjoy them in a stir-fry or a salad, these baby soybeans have 9 grams of protein per ½ cup.

5. Black beans: My favorite taco ingredient supplies nearly 8 grams of protein per ½-cup serving.

6. Quinoa: Not only does quinoa have 8 grams of protein per cup, it's also a complete protein, meaning it contains all the essential amino acids your body needs.

7. Greek yogurt: From breakfast to frozen-yogurt bites, 1 cup of Greek yogurt delivers 17 grams of protein.

8. Chickpea pasta: This is one of my favorite swaps for white-flour pasta. It tastes like whole-wheat pasta but has more protein and fiber and fewer carbohydrates.

9. Chia seeds: Whether I'm tossing them into my overnight oats or blending them into my smoothies, chia seeds are a great protein boost, with 4 grams in just 2 tablespoons.

10. Hemp seeds: I often sprinkle these on my yogurt bowls or smoothies, because 3 tablespoons of hemp seeds contain 10 grams of protein.

HEALTHY FATS

We've all heard the term *healthy fats*, but let's talk about what that really means. Mono-unsaturated fats and polyunsaturated fats are known as "good fats" because they're the fats that can help lower your LDL cholesterol (the bad cholesterol) and raise your HDL cholesterol (the good stuff). These fats have also been associated with lowering blood pressure.

Polyunsaturated fats are found in a lot of nuts and seeds, like walnuts and sunflower seeds. Monounsaturated fats are found in things like olive oil and avocados. In fact, avocados are a great source of both monounsaturated and polyunsaturated fats. They're actually made up of 77 percent fat, which is why they're dense in terms of calories. Luckily, you need only a few slices to get both the flavor and the health benefits. Peanut butter is also a good source of monounsaturated and polyunsaturated fats. Get rid of the reduced-fat peanut butter and go for the real thing. I love having a scoop of peanut butter with apple slices, or a spoonful blended right into a smoothie.

Omega-3 fatty acids are a certain type of polyunsaturated fat that's especially beneficial to your health. They can reduce inflammation in the body and even lower your triglycerides, which have been linked to heart disease. Omega-3s can be found in chia seeds, walnuts, edamame, kale, spinach, and more.

COMPLEX CARBS

While a vegetarian diet might not be particularly low-carb, it's important to recognize that not all carbs are created equal. *Simple carbohydrates* are easy-to-digest basic sugars. These could be naturally occurring in things like fruit, but they're also the added sugars that you'll find in everything from baked goods to bottled salad dressings. You've probably also heard of *refined carbohydrates*, which include any carb-based food that has been processed—things like white rice, sugar, and white flour. These refined carbohydrates

Healthy Cooking Oils

You'll notice that most of the recipes in this book use olive oil, but occasionally a recipe calls for avocado oil. Avocado oil and olive oil are similar in terms of health benefits, but avocado oil can be cooked at a higher heat, and it has a neutral flavor that works well in baking and cooking. Olive oil is great for salads and roasted vegetables, but when it comes to sweet salad dressings or cooking at a high heat, avocado oil is the better choice.

give you a quick and immediate burst of energy, but then you might feel a crash a few hours later.

The recipes in this book focus on *complex carbohydrates*, such as beans, whole grains, and vegetables. Complex carbohydrates give you a slow release of energy, so there's no crash later on, and they provide fiber, which helps with digestion. These are the carbohydrates that will fill you up, keep you satisfied, and give your body the fuel it needs throughout the day. In this book, I focus on a balance of complex carbohydrates, healthy fats, and proteins to keep you nourished and energized.

MIX-AND-MATCH HEALTHY MEALS

Incorporating whole foods into your diet can sound intimidating at first, but once you learn a few simple recipes, you'll start to get the hang of it. This book will teach you plenty of recipes that you can make as written, but oftentimes I find myself mixing and matching based on whatever I have in the kitchen. As long as you have a few basics in your pantry, you can put together delicious and healthy meals.

For example, I usually have chickpeas, zucchini, and avocado at all times. One evening I might make roasted chickpeas with zucchini fries. The next day I'll make a sandwich using mashed chickpeas and avocado. The following day I might make Zucchini Noodles (page 24) with avocado pesto. As you get more familiar with these ingredients, you might even start creating your own recipes.

Helpful Kitchen Equipment

Learning to eat in a new way or figuring out new methods for preparing food can feel challenging at first, but with the right tools in the kitchen, making these recipes will be a breeze. There are a few must-haves that I can't recommend enough. I also share some of my favorite nice-to-have kitchen equipment.

Many of these must-have items are probably already in your kitchen. If not, consider investing in these tools, because you'll need them for the recipes in this book.

Sharp knife: Having a sharp knife is essential when preparing fruits and vegetables.

Knife sharpener: Even the sharpest knife gets dull after a while. You can find a small manual knife sharpener for less than $20.

Large pot: You'll need a pot that holds at least 8 quarts of liquid to make soups and stews.

Nonstick skillet: While I love a cast-iron skillet, I find that a nonstick skillet is so much handier. A nonstick surface means you won't need to add a lot of oil during cooking.

Nonstick baking sheet: A 13-by-9-inch nonstick baking sheet is perfect for roasting vegetables and baking cookies. (Parchment paper is great for creating a nonstick surface on baking sheets you already have, and makes cleanup a breeze.)

Getting Enough Iron

Protein tends to get a lot of attention, but getting enough iron can be a bigger challenge for vegetarians or people who eat mostly vegetarian. While there are plenty of plant-based sources of iron, typically the iron in plant foods isn't as easily absorbed as the iron in animal-based foods. This means it's important to make sure you're incorporating plenty of foods that are good sources of iron.

Here are my 10 favorite plant-based sources of iron:

Vitamin C can help encourage iron absorption. Some studies have found that combining vitamin C with a plant-based source of iron can increase absorption up to 300 percent. The best part is, foods high in vitamin C pair well with a lot of these iron sources. For example, adding tomato salsa to your rice and beans is a great way to add vitamin C (from the tomatoes) to your meal and makes it easier for your body to absorb the iron in the beans.

1. Beans
2. Lentils
3. Tofu
4. Tempeh
5. Hemp seeds
6. Cashews
7. Pine nuts
8. Mushrooms
9. Quinoa
10. Cocoa

Nonstick muffin pan: A nonstick or silicone muffin pan will help your healthy muffins slide right out—no need to worry about them sticking to the sides. It's good to have one 12-cup muffin pan and one mini muffin pan.

Vegetable peeler: Not only is a good peeler handy for prepping vegetables, but you can also use it to make vegetable noodles.

Blender: Whether you're whipping up sauces or just saving time chopping vegetables, a powerful blender makes prep work so much easier.

NICE-TO-HAVES

These items are optional, but they've become some of my favorites.

Spiralizer: This handy tool makes it quick and easy to transform my vegetables into noodles. This is definitely optional, but fun!

Food processor: While a blender can be used for the recipes in this book, I love how quickly a food processor can chop onions, shred carrots, and finely mince garlic. You can even make your own nut butters in a food processor.

Cast-iron skillet: Cast-iron skillets tend to be an investment, but for good reason. They can literally last a lifetime, and they're great for uniform cooking temperatures. They can also go from the stove top to the oven.

Rice cooker: A rice cooker makes it easy to prepare a big batch of not just rice but any grain without having to keep a close eye on it. I make a lot of quinoa, which cooks perfectly in a rice cooker.

Mandoline: A mandoline slicer makes it easy to cut produce into thin, uniform slices at a quick pace. It's handy for salads or dishes that require lots of sliced vegetables.

About the Recipes

All of the recipes in this book are designed to be truly healthy. That's why you won't see any processed ingredients; instead, you'll find a healthy balance of whole foods for delicious, nourishing meals. Many of these dishes contain grains and beans, but those won't necessarily be the stars of the show. Grains and beans do provide protein and fiber, but I balance out their carbohydrates with other healthy ingredients.

Here's what you'll find in each recipe:

Yield: Don't forget to keep an eye on serving sizes. Each recipe includes the yield at the top. Remember that if you eat half a dish that was meant to serve four people, it might not be healthy anymore. I share some of my favorite quick snack suggestions, too, so if you need a little something between meals, be sure to check those out.

Prep and cook times: To make healthy eating as easy as possible, many of these recipes can be made in 30 minutes or less from start to finish. I personally don't like having to spend my whole evening prepping meals, so most of these recipes are quick as well as easy.

Equipment: I note what pots and pans you'll need to cook the recipe, plus any appliances and special tools. Some recipes use only one pan. I hate washing dishes, and I'll bet you do, too.

Ingredients: Some recipes call for only five or fewer ingredients, and none have a huge list.

Cooking instructions: I explain everything step-by-step, and I keep it simple.

Tips: I give you some ideas for ingredient substitutions, suggestions on what can be made ahead of time, tips on prep, information about ingredients, and even some ways to add meat to some of these dishes (I call those "flexitarian tips").

Labels: All of these recipes are vegetarian, but they also have a label to indicate when they're dairy-free, gluten-free, low-carb (fewer than 30 grams per serving), nut-free, soy-free, or vegan. When possible, I provide substitutions to fit your preferred eating style.

Vegetable-Based "Pasta" and "Rice"

Zucchini Noodles (page 24) and Cauliflower Rice (page 25) have exploded in popularity as lower-carb alternatives to some of our favorite comfort foods. This is partly because things like pasta and rice don't really taste like much on their own; it's all about the sauces. Vegetables actually have more flavor, and with the right spices and seasonings, you can transform vegetables into a delicious base for some fantastic meals. This book includes plenty of recipes that use whole-grain pasta and brown rice (check out chapter 9), but I also share with you some of my favorite lower-carb swaps.

For example, I love pasta with pesto sauce. My Pesto Zucchini Noodles (page 117) has just 12 grams of carbs, compared with 48 grams of carbs in regular pasta. Cauliflower Rice (page 25) makes a great base for burrito bowls and stir-fries, and spaghetti squash is the key to one of my favorite "pasta" recipes. (Try the Red Lentil Bolognese on page 118!) Once you find your favorite vegetable-based grain swaps, you might find yourself using them all the time.

It's easy to fall back on convenience foods when you're looking for a quick snack, but they're often full of sugar, carbs, and processed ingredients. Here's a selection of super-easy, healthy snacks you can throw together in less than 10 minutes.

1. **Green Smoothie:** 1 frozen banana blended with ½ cup ice, ½ cup almond milk, ½ cup spinach, and 1 tablespoon peanut butter

2. **Cinnamon Apple Slices:** 1 apple, thinly sliced, sprinkled with cinnamon, and dipped in 1 tablespoon peanut butter

3. **Crunchy Greek Yogurt:** 1 cup Greek yogurt topped with 2 tablespoons sliced almonds

4. **Spicy Avocado Toast:** 1 slice whole-grain toast topped with ½ avocado and ¼ teaspoon red pepper flakes

5. **Banana Roll-Up:** ½ banana and 2 teaspoons peanut butter, rolled up in 1 whole-grain tortilla

6. **Bell Pepper Dippers:** 1 cup bell pepper strips dipped in 2 tablespoons guacamole

7. **Strawberries and Peanut Butter Dip:** 1 cup strawberries, served with 3 tablespoons Greek yogurt mixed with 2 teaspoons peanut butter

8. **Cucumber Rolls:** 1 cucumber, thinly sliced lengthwise into 10 strips, each topped with 1 teaspoon hummus and a pinch of paprika, and rolled up

9. **Sweet and Salty Popcorn:** 1 cup air-popped popcorn tossed with 2 tablespoons walnuts and 2 teaspoons dried cranberries

10. **Cucumbers and Tzatziki Dip:** 1 cup sliced cucumber, dipped in ½ cup Greek yogurt mixed with 1 teaspoon olive oil and ¼ teaspoon dried dill

11. **Avocado Egg Salad:** 1 hardboiled egg, diced, mixed with ½ avocado, diced, and seasoned with salt and pepper

12. **Ricotta Toast:** 1 slice whole-grain toast topped with ¼ cup ricotta cheese, a handful of blackberries, and a drizzle of honey

13. **Easy Frozen Yogurt:** ½ cup Greek yogurt blended with ½ cup frozen mango (it tastes like frozen yogurt!)

14. **Almond Butter Bites:** 6 whole-grain crackers, each topped with ½ teaspoon almond butter and 1 raspberry

15. **Sweet and Savory Pears:** 6 slices pear, each topped with 1 teaspoon goat cheese and a few almond slices and drizzled with honey, if desired

Nutritional information: Each recipe lists the calories, fat, carbs, fiber, sugar, protein, and sodium per serving, in case those are numbers you need to count.

I hope this book will help you eat healthier and save you time in the kitchen. Be sure to try out a few things that might sound unfamiliar, and push yourself to explore new cooking styles. My husband and I enjoy these recipes on our own and with friends and family, so I'm thrilled for you to try them in your kitchen.

Avocado Ranch Dressing, page 20

CHAPTER 2

Basics

There are a handful of recipes that I find myself making over and over again because they're such perfect staples. I love making my own salad dressings and seasoning blends because it helps me save a few bucks at the grocery store and I know exactly what ingredients are in my food. You'll often find that things like bottled salad dressings are loaded with sugar and not-so-heart-healthy oils. These basics are the building blocks for some of the recipes throughout this book, so use this section as a handy reference.

Taco Seasoning

MAKES ¼ CUP [½ TABLESPOON = 1 SERVING]
PREP TIME: 5 minutes

This taco seasoning works well on black beans, lentils, cauliflower, or anything you can stuff inside a taco. It's just spicy enough to give a kick of flavor without overpowering the rest of your dish. Of course, you can dial up the spice if you like, but I recommend starting with this blend and adding more heat to your final dish. This seasoning can be stored for months in your pantry, but I doubt it will last that long.

2 tablespoons chili powder

1 teaspoon garlic powder

1 teaspoon onion powder

½ teaspoon dried oregano

1 teaspoon paprika

2 teaspoons cumin

2 teaspoons salt

1. In a small jar, combine the chili powder, garlic powder, onion powder, oregano, paprika, cumin, and salt.

2. Stir, or shake with the lid on, to combine.

3. Store in an airtight jar or container for up to 3 months.

DAIRY-FREE • GLUTEN-FREE • LOW-CARB
NUT-FREE • SOY-FREE • VEGAN

Per ½-tablespoon serving: Calories: 11; Fat: 1g; Carbs: 2g; Fiber: 1g; Sugar: 0g; Protein: 1g; Sodium: 602mg

Easy Greek Salad Dressing

This is such a simple combination of flavors, but it's delicious on a salad of crunchy romaine lettuce, cucumbers, tomatoes, red onions, and feta cheese. Or try it over a simple salad of mixed greens. However you decide to use it, this great dressing is easy to whip up with pantry staples.

⅓ cup olive oil

¼ cup balsamic vinegar

¼ teaspoon garlic powder

¼ teaspoon dried oregano

¼ teaspoon dried parsley

¼ teaspoon salt

1. In a medium bowl, whisk together the olive oil, vinegar, garlic powder, oregano, parsley, and salt.

2. Store in an airtight container in the refrigerator for up to 1 week.

Prep tip: This dressing will separate after it sits for a bit, so I usually just give it a good shake before using. But if you want to prevent the oil and vinegar from separating, you can whisk in 1 tablespoon mayonnaise to emulsify the dressing.

DAIRY-FREE • GLUTEN-FREE • LOW-CARB
NUT-FREE • SOY-FREE • VEGAN

Per 2-tablespoon serving: Calories: 74; Fat: 8g; Carbs: 0g; Fiber: 0g; Sugar: 0g; Protein: 0g; Sodium: 74mg

Garlic-Almond Dressing

MAKES 1 CUP [2 TABLESPOONS = 1 SERVING]
EQUIPMENT: Blender or food processor
PREP TIME: 10 minutes

This garlic-almond dressing has a creamy, tangy flavor that might remind you of a Caesar dressing, but it's much healthier. I love it served on top of crisp romaine lettuce or hearty kale. The flavor also works well with any mild, crunchy vegetables, like cucumbers, carrots, and peppers, so whip up this dressing and serve it with whatever veggies you have in the refrigerator.

¼ cup almond flour

1 teaspoon whole-grain mustard

4 garlic cloves

2 tablespoons freshly squeezed lemon juice

3 tablespoons olive oil

½ teaspoon salt, plus more if needed

¼ cup water, plus more if needed

1. Blend the almond flour, mustard, garlic, lemon juice, olive oil, salt, and water in a blender or food processor until creamy.

2. Add more water to thin the dressing if needed. Taste and add more salt if needed.

3. Store in the refrigerator for up to 1 week.

Ingredient tip: Almond flour is made from ground almonds. It can usually be found with the gluten-free flours at the grocery store or in health food stores.

DAIRY-FREE • GLUTEN-FREE • LOW-CARB
SOY-FREE • VEGAN

Per 2-tablespoon serving: Calories: 55; Fat: 6g; Carbs: 1g; Fiber: 0g; Sugar: 0g; Protein: 0g; Sodium: 161mg

Sweet Poppy Seed Dressing

MAKES 1 CUP [2 TABLESPOONS = 1 SERVING]
EQUIPMENT: Blender or food processor
PREP TIME: 10 minutes

For years I thought poppy seeds were some sort of exotic food, until I realized that they're sold in the spice section of most supermarkets, right by the pepper. Now I make my own poppy seed dressing at home. This salad dressing might become your favorite in the summertime, because it lends itself to lighter greens, like spinach, and fruity toppings such as apples and mandarin oranges.

¼ cup plain Greek yogurt

¼ cup apple cider vinegar

2 tablespoons honey

1 teaspoon Dijon mustard

½ teaspoon salt

¼ cup avocado oil

1 tablespoon poppy seeds

1. Blend the yogurt, vinegar, honey, mustard, salt, and avocado oil in a blender or food processor until smooth.

2. Transfer to a small jar and stir in the poppy seeds.

3. Store in the refrigerator for up to 3 days.

Ingredient tip: I like using avocado oil in this recipe because it has a neutral flavor and similar health benefits to olive oil. If you don't want to add a new oil to your pantry, you can use olive oil here, but it will have a slightly more savory flavor.

GLUTEN-FREE • LOW-CARB • NUT-FREE • SOY-FREE
DAIRY-FREE: *Substitute almond milk yogurt or soy milk yogurt for the Greek yogurt.*
VEGAN: *Go dairy-free, and use agave nectar instead of honey.*

Per 2-tablespoon serving: Calories: 91; Fat: 8g; Carbs: 5g; Fiber: 0g; Sugar: 5g; Protein: 1g; Sodium: 158mg

Avocado Ranch Dressing

MAKES 1 CUP [2 TABLESPOONS = 1 SERVING]
EQUIPMENT: Blender or food processor
PREP TIME: 10 minutes

I was raised in the Midwest, which means I grew up on ranch dressing. This avocado ranch dressing is a healthier version of that classic favorite. It still has a creamy tang, thanks to the Greek yogurt, but it's full of healthy fats and a little added protein.

1 large avocado

¼ cup plain nonfat Greek yogurt

2 teaspoons freshly squeezed lemon juice

1 small garlic clove

½ teaspoon dried parsley

½ teaspoon dried dill

½ teaspoon dried chives

½ teaspoon onion powder

¼ teaspoon salt

½ cup almond milk

1. Slice the avocado in half and discard the pit.

2. Scoop the avocado flesh into a blender or food processor.

3. Add the yogurt, lemon juice, garlic, parsley, dill, chives, onion powder, salt, and almond milk, and blend until smooth.

4. Serve immediately.

GLUTEN-FREE • LOW-CARB • SOY-FREE
DAIRY-FREE: *Substitute Greek-style almond milk yogurt for the Greek yogurt.*

Per 2-tablespoon serving: Calories: 91; Fat: 9g; Carbs: 4g; Fiber: 2g; Sugar: 1g; Protein: 2g; Sodium: 81mg

Spicy Peanut Sauce

This peanut sauce is perfect on rice noodles and stir-fried vegetables or served with fresh spring rolls. It's easy to whip up ahead of time, so I like to make a double batch and store it in a mason jar.

¼ cup honey

2 tablespoons creamy peanut butter

¼ cup low-sodium soy sauce

½ teaspoon red curry paste

1. In a large bowl, whisk together the honey, peanut butter, soy sauce, and curry paste.

2. Store in an airtight container in the refrigerator for up to 1 week.

Substitution tip: Red curry paste can be found in the Asian section of most grocery stores. If you can't find it, feel free to substitute ½ teaspoon sriracha or another hot sauce.

DAIRY-FREE • LOW-CARB
GLUTEN-FREE: *Use gluten-free tamari instead of soy sauce.*
VEGAN: *Use agave nectar instead of honey.*

Per 2-tablespoon serving: Calories: 59; Fat: 2g; Carbs: 10g; Fiber: 0g; Sugar: 10g; Protein: 2g; Sodium: 475mg

Enchilada Sauce

MAKES 2 CUPS [¼ CUP = 1 SERVING]
EQUIPMENT: Small saucepan
PREP TIME: 10 minutes
COOK TIME: 5 minutes

I could practically eat this Enchilada Sauce with a spoon. I came up with this recipe when I was craving enchiladas and wanted to avoid running to the store to buy a jar of sauce. It turned out to be so easy and I loved the flavor, so now I make this regularly.

2 tablespoons olive oil

2 tablespoons whole-wheat flour

2 tablespoons chili powder

2 cups low-sodium vegetable broth

2½ tablespoons tomato paste

¼ teaspoon cayenne pepper

1 teaspoon ground cumin

Salt

1. In a small saucepan, stir together the olive oil, flour, and chili powder. Cook over medium heat for 2 to 3 minutes until the mixture begins to bubble.

2. Whisk in the vegetable broth, tomato paste, cayenne pepper, and cumin.

3. Let the sauce simmer for 1 minute until it starts to thicken.

4. Remove from the heat and season with salt to taste.

Make-ahead tip: This Enchilada Sauce can be made up to 1 week in advance. Just store it in the refrigerator in an airtight container until you're ready to use it.

DAIRY-FREE • LOW-CARB • NUT-FREE
SOY-FREE • VEGAN
GLUTEN-FREE: *Substitute any gluten-free flour.*

Per ¼-cup serving: Calories: 58; Fat: 4g; Carbs: 4g; Fiber: 1g; Sugar: 1g; Protein: 2g; Sodium: 362mg

Collard Green Wraps

SERVES 4
EQUIPMENT: Large pot
PREP TIME: 5 minutes
COOK TIME: 5 minutes

Move aside, lettuce wraps—these collard greens are an amazingly versatile way to wrap your favorite fillings. Their wide leaves make it easy to roll up your lunch like a burrito, and they take only a few minutes to prepare. This recipe calls for Quinoa Tabbouleh (page 73), but stuff these wraps with whatever you like!

4 large collard green leaves

1 cup store-bought roasted red pepper hummus

2 cups Quinoa Tabbouleh (page 73)

Ingredient tip: When choosing collard greens, look for large leaves with no tears or holes. You can eat them raw, but steaming them first will make them softer and more pliable.

1. Bring a large pot of water to a boil and gently steam the leaves over the pot, one at a time, for 10 to 20 seconds each. Use tongs to hold each leaf over the pot, or simply grab it by the stem. (Keep your hands out of the column of steam! You may want to wear an oven mitt.)

2. After steaming, pat the leaves with a paper towel to remove any excess moisture.

3. Trim the stem of each leaf at its base so it is even with the bottom of the leaf, as this will make it easier to roll. Depending on how thick the stem is, you can trim off more of it. Just make sure you leave at least half the leaf intact.

4. Spread ¼ cup of hummus on the wide part of the leaf and top with ½ cup of Quinoa Tabbouleh. Starting from the wide end, roll up each wrap, tucking in the sides like a burrito as you go. Be sure not to roll too tightly or the wrap will tear. Repeat with the remaining collard greens and filling.

5. Serve immediately.

DAIRY-FREE • GLUTEN-FREE • LOW-CARB
NUT-FREE • SOY-FREE • VEGAN

Per wrap (without filling): Calories: 25; Fat: 0g; Carbs: 5g; Fiber: 3g; Sugar: 0g; Protein: 2g; Sodium: 15mg

Zucchini Noodles

SERVES 4

EQUIPMENT: Spiralizer, mandoline, or vegetable peeler; large nonstick skillet

PREP TIME: 15 minutes

COOK TIME: 5 minutes

Making noodles out of zucchini is one of my favorite ways to enjoy a low-carb dinner while still getting the satisfying feeling of comfort food. A spiralizer makes it fun to turn all sorts of vegetables into noodles, but a good old-fashioned vegetable peeler works just as well. To make sure that you don't end up with a watery mess, follow this recipe closely.

4 medium zucchini

Salt

1 teaspoon olive oil

1. Slice the ends off the zucchini so you have a flat surface on each end. Spiralize into strands, cutting them every 6 inches. If you don't have a spiralizer, use a mandoline or a vegetable peeler to shave the zucchini into thin ribbons.

2. Discard the "seedy" strands. These come from the center of the zucchini and have a high water content, which can make the rest of your strands soggy.

3. Sprinkle the noodles with a pinch of salt and let them sit in a colander for at least 10 minutes to help get rid of some of the excess moisture.

4. In a large nonstick skillet over medium heat, sauté the zucchini with the olive oil for 2 to 3 minutes. Be careful not to overcook or the noodles will get soggy. Drain any excess moisture from the bottom of the skillet.

5. Add your favorite sauce or seasoning and toss with the noodles. Serve immediately.

DAIRY-FREE • GLUTEN-FREE • LOW-CARB
NUT-FREE • SOY-FREE • VEGAN

Per serving: Calories: 41; Fat: 2g; Carbs: 7g; Fiber: 2g; Sugar: 3g; Protein: 2g; Sodium: 58mg

Cauliflower Rice

SERVES 4

EQUIPMENT: Box grater or food processor, large nonstick skillet

PREP TIME: 15 minutes

COOK TIME: 10 minutes

Cauliflower is an amazing replacement for white rice. When prepared correctly, it's a nearly identical swap that has fewer carbs and does a great job of absorbing flavors. I love using it in recipes like stuffed peppers and stir-fries. Try this healthy rice alternative in your next taco.

1 large head cauliflower

1 tablespoon olive oil

1. Tear off any green leaves that are still on the cauliflower. Then, using a sharp knife, chop the head into 4 large pieces.

2. Using a box grater, grate the cauliflower into rice-size bits. This can be a bit messy, so it helps to do this over a large bowl. Or you can finely chop it in a food processor.

3. Heat the olive oil in a large nonstick skillet over medium heat. Add the cauliflower and cook for 5 to 7 minutes, stirring frequently, until it starts to soften.

4. Drain any excess moisture from the skillet.

5. Add any seasoning you like and serve immediately.

Prep tip: If you have the patience, use a box grater rather than a food processor. I find it produces more uniform pieces.

DAIRY-FREE · GLUTEN-FREE · LOW-CARB
NUT-FREE · SOY-FREE · VEGAN

Per serving: Calories: 83; Fat: 4g; Carbs: 11g; Fiber: 5g; Sugar: 5g; Protein: 4g; Sodium: 63mg

Roasted Chickpeas

SERVES 4
EQUIPMENT: Baking sheet
PREP TIME: 5 minutes
COOK TIME: 25 minutes

Roasted chickpeas are one of my all-time favorite foods. That might sound odd, but chickpeas are irresistible when they're roasted until crispy. I always have a can of chickpeas in the pantry, so this is an easy dish to serve with roasted vegetables or a salad on a busy weeknight. You can play around with adding any spices you like. In my family, we love a sprinkle of garlic, chili powder, and cumin.

2 (15-ounce) cans chickpeas, drained and rinsed

1 tablespoon olive oil

½ teaspoon salt

Garlic powder, cumin, chili powder, or any spices you like

1. Preheat the oven to 450°F.

2. In a large bowl, toss the chickpeas and olive oil together until the chickpeas are lightly coated. Sprinkle with the salt and any other spices you'd like to use.

3. Line a baking sheet with parchment paper and spread the chickpeas out in a single layer.

4. Bake for 15 minutes, then stir the chickpeas and continue to bake for 5 to 10 minutes more until the chickpeas are browned and crispy.

DAIRY-FREE • GLUTEN-FREE • NUT-FREE
SOY-FREE • VEGAN

Per serving: Calories: 316; Fat: 6g; Carbs: 54g; Fiber: 11g; Sugar: 0g; Protein: 12g; Sodium: 1008mg

Whole-Wheat Flatbreads

SERVES 4

EQUIPMENT: Large nonstick skillet
PREP TIME: 20 minutes
COOK TIME: 10 minutes

Sure, you could buy flatbread at the store, but you can also make your own at home—and it's *so* simple. These flatbreads are 100 percent whole-wheat with no added sugars or preservatives, so you know exactly what you're getting in your flatbread. I know there's something intimidating about making your own bread from scratch, but don't be afraid. Try this once and you'll see how easy it is.

⅔ cup warm water

1 teaspoon salt

¼ cup olive oil

2 cups white whole-wheat flour

Pinch dried herbs (rosemary, basil, oregano, or others; optional)

Ingredient tip: White whole-wheat flour is simply a type of whole-wheat flour. It's still packed with fiber, protein, vitamins, and minerals, but it has a milder flavor than traditional whole-wheat flour. If you don't have any, you can still make this recipe with regular whole-wheat flour, but it will have a slightly chewier texture.

1. In a large bowl, stir together the warm water and salt until the salt dissolves. Stir in the olive oil. Add the flour and work it with your hands until the moisture is distributed and the dough comes together.

2. Knead the dough in the bowl for 3 to 4 minutes. Let it rest for 15 minutes.

3. Cut the dough into 4 pieces. Place each piece between two sheets of parchment paper and use a rolling pin to roll it as thin as possible. It'll puff up while cooking, so try to roll it into a very thin sheet. Sprinkle with the herbs, if using.

4. Heat a large nonstick skillet over medium heat and cook each piece for 2 to 3 minutes per side. You won't need any oil—as long as you use a nonstick pan, you shouldn't have any trouble flipping the flatbreads. Be sure not to overcook or they'll get crispy.

5. Let cool and store in an airtight container until you're ready to use them.

DAIRY-FREE • LOW-CARB • NUT-FREE
SOY-FREE • VEGAN
GLUTEN-FREE: *Swap in any gluten-free flour.*

Per serving: Calories: 158; Fat: 13g; Carbs: 11g; Fiber: 2g; Sugar: 1g; Protein: 2g; Sodium: 581mg

Coconut-Mango Smoothie, page 31

CHAPTER 3

Breakfasts

When you start with a healthy breakfast, it gives your body energy throughout the day. I find that if I eat healthy in the morning, I'm more likely to make healthy choices all day. Whether you're looking for something quick and easy to make on your way out the door or you need a healthy recipe that you can serve for brunch, these meals will keep you satisfied until lunchtime.

Green Tea Smoothie

SERVES 1
EQUIPMENT: Blender
PREP TIME: 5 minutes

I love this smoothie during the warm summer months because it's so light and refreshing. The green tea adds flavor without adding sugar. For a twist, substitute frozen mango for the frozen peaches.

3 large ice cubes

¾ cup frozen peach chunks

⅓ cup green tea, cooled

¼ cup plain Greek yogurt

1 teaspoon honey

1. Add the ice cubes, peaches, green tea, yogurt, and honey to a blender and blend until smooth.

2. Pour into a large glass and drink right away.

Ingredient tip: Green tea contains caffeine, so this is a great smoothie to perk you up in the morning.

GLUTEN-FREE • LOW-CARB • NUT-FREE • SOY-FREE
DAIRY-FREE: *Use coconut milk yogurt or almond milk yogurt instead of Greek yogurt.*
VEGAN: *Go dairy-free, and substitute maple syrup or agave nectar for the honey.*

Per serving: Calories: 106; Fat: 1g; Carbs: 19g; Fiber: 2g; Sugar: 17g; Protein: 7g; Sodium: 25mg

Coconut-Mango Smoothie

SERVES 2
EQUIPMENT: Blender
PREP TIME: 5 minutes

This is one of my all-time favorite smoothie combinations. It tastes like my favorite frozen yogurt, but since the mango and pineapple are already sweet, it doesn't require any additional sweetener.

1 cup ice cubes

1 cup frozen mango chunks

1 cup frozen pineapple chunks

1 cup unsweetened coconut milk or almond milk

2 tablespoons unsweetened coconut flakes

1 tablespoon chia seeds (optional)

1. Blend the ice, mango, pineapple, and coconut milk or almond milk in a blender until smooth.

2. Divide between two glasses and sprinkle with the coconut flakes and chia seeds (if using).

Ingredient tip: Chia seeds contain lots of fiber and healthy fats, which can help balance blood sugar. They are a great addition to smoothies like this one, which contains natural sugars from the fruit. You can find them at many supermarkets and health food stores.

DAIRY-FREE • GLUTEN-FREE • NUT-FREE
SOY-FREE • VEGAN

Per serving: Calories: 263; Fat: 10g; Carbs: 41g; Fiber: 5g; Sugar: 36g; Protein: 2g; Sodium: 88mg

Banana Overnight Oats

If your mornings always feel busy or chaotic, these overnight oats are for you. You can prep them the night before and then grab them to go on your way out the door. Customize them with your favorite toppings, or keep things simple with a little peanut butter. The chia seeds help thicken up the oats overnight, but they also provide protein and fiber to keep you full and energized all morning long.

1 banana

1 cup unsweetened almond milk

1 cup rolled oats

2 tablespoons chopped walnuts

2 tablespoons chia seeds

2 tablespoons maple syrup

1 teaspoon ground cinnamon

2 tablespoons peanut butter (optional)

1. In a medium bowl, mash the banana with a fork. Add the almond milk, oats, walnuts, chia seeds, maple syrup, and cinnamon. Mash until combined.

2. Divide the mixture between two jars with tight-fitting lids.

3. Let chill in the refrigerator for at least 6 hours or overnight.

4. Top with the peanut butter (if using) just before serving.

Make-ahead tip: This recipe makes enough for two servings, but you don't have to eat them right away. Store the second jar for breakfast the following day!

DAIRY-FREE • SOY-FREE • VEGAN

GLUTEN-FREE: *Use gluten-free oats.*

Per serving: Calories: 332; Fat: 15g; Carbs: 50g; Fiber: 11g; Sugar: 20g; Protein: 9g; Sodium: 183mg

Grain-Free Granola

MAKES 2 CUPS [¼ CUP = 1 SERVING]
EQUIPMENT: Nonstick baking sheet
PREP TIME: 10 minutes
COOK TIME: 15 minutes

Store-bought granola is often loaded with sugar, unlike this super satisfying homemade version. Although the fat content might seem high, it's coming from the almonds and coconut, which provide protein and fiber. Plus, since it's low in sugar, you don't have to worry about an energy crash an hour later! This recipe is for 8 servings, so it's perfect for making ahead of time. Just store in an airtight container and scoop some out whenever you want to add a bit of crunch to your yogurt or oatmeal.

3 tablespoons coconut oil

¼ teaspoon pure vanilla extract

1 tablespoon honey

1 cup unsweetened coconut flakes

1 cup sliced almonds

Pinch salt

1. Preheat the oven to 300°F.

2. Pour the coconut oil into a small microwave-safe bowl and heat for 30 seconds, until melted, or melt in a small pan on the stove top over low heat. Stir in the vanilla and honey.

3. In a large bowl, combine the coconut flakes, almonds, and salt. Drizzle with the coconut oil mixture and stir to coat.

4. Spread the granola in a single layer on a nonstick baking sheet. You can leave it a little chunky if you like clumps in your granola.

5. Bake for 10 to 12 minutes until the coconut begins to brown.

6. Let cool completely before removing from the baking sheet.

DAIRY-FREE • GLUTEN-FREE • LOW-CARB • SOY-FREE
VEGAN: *Substitute maple syrup for the honey.*

Per serving: Calories: 200; Fat: 18g; Carbs: 8g; Fiber: 4g; Sugar: 4g; Protein: 3g; Sodium: 24mg

Peanut Butter and Quinoa Breakfast Bowl

SERVES 2
EQUIPMENT: Medium saucepan
PREP TIME: 10 minutes
COOK TIME: 5 minutes

If you love oatmeal, give this quinoa bowl a try. It has a similar flavor profile with a slightly different texture. Feel free to play around with additional toppings. Sometimes I trade the peanut butter and banana for cinnamon and raisins.

1 cup cooked quinoa

¼ cup unsweetened almond milk

2 teaspoons honey

½ teaspoon pure vanilla extract

1 banana, sliced

2 tablespoons peanut butter

1. In a medium saucepan over medium heat, combine the quinoa and almond milk and heat for 2 minutes.

2. Add the honey and vanilla and stir until combined.

3. Remove from the heat and divide between two bowls.

4. Top with the banana and peanut butter and serve.

DAIRY-FREE • GLUTEN-FREE • SOY-FREE
VEGAN: *Use maple syrup instead of honey.*

Per serving: Calories: 307; Fat: 11g; Carbs: 45g; Fiber: 6g; Sugar: 16g; Protein: 10g; Sodium: 129mg

Pumpkin Almond Flour Muffins

MAKES 8 MUFFINS [1 MUFFIN = 1 SERVING]
EQUIPMENT: 8- or 12-cup nonstick muffin pan
PREP TIME: 10 minutes
COOK TIME: 25 minutes

If you've never baked with almond flour, try it with these muffins! Almond flour has just 24 grams of carbohydrates per cup, compared with 86 grams in whole-wheat flour. But although almond flour is low-carb, it's not low-calorie. If you want to lower the calorie count, leave out the pecans. Also, make sure you use plain pumpkin purée, not pumpkin pie filling, which has added spices and sugar.

⅔ cup pumpkin purée

2 large eggs

¼ cup honey

1 tablespoon coconut oil, melted, at room temperature

1 teaspoon pure vanilla extract

1⅓ cups almond flour

1 teaspoon baking powder

1 teaspoon baking soda

1 teaspoon ground cinnamon

¼ teaspoon ground ginger

½ teaspoon salt

½ cup finely chopped pecans

Nonstick cooking spray

1. Preheat the oven to 350°F.

2. In a large bowl, combine the pumpkin purée and eggs. Mix in the honey, coconut oil, and vanilla.

3. In another large bowl, combine the almond flour, baking powder, baking soda, cinnamon, ginger, salt, and pecans.

4. Add the almond flour mixture to the pumpkin mixture and stir until just combined. The batter will be lumpy.

5. Spray a nonstick muffin pan with nonstick cooking spray. Evenly fill 8 muffin cups with the batter.

6. Bake for 19 to 22 minutes until browned on the edges and set in the middle.

7. Let sit for 2 minutes, then remove the muffins from the pan and cool on a cooling rack.

Prep tip: Be sure to remove the muffins from the pan. They can become soggy if left in the pan, because the cups trap the escaping steam.

DAIRY-FREE • GLUTEN-FREE • LOW-CARB • SOY-FREE

Per muffin: Calories: 150; Fat: 10g; Carbs: 13g; Fiber: 2g; Sugar: 10g; Protein: 4g; Sodium: 327mg

Greek Yogurt and Banana Muffins

MAKES 12 MUFFINS [1 MUFFIN = 1 SERVING]
EQUIPMENT: 12-cup nonstick muffin pan
PREP TIME: 35 minutes
COOK TIME: 20 minutes

These banana muffins have an amazingly fluffy texture, thanks to the Greek yogurt. You can substitute regular whole-wheat flour for the pastry flour, but pastry flour will result in a lighter muffin. As for the mix-ins, you can customize these with whatever you like.

Nonstick cooking spray

3 small or 2 large very ripe bananas

¼ cup honey

1 egg

¼ cup almond milk

½ cup plain Greek yogurt

1 teaspoon pure vanilla extract

1½ cups whole-wheat pastry flour

1 teaspoon baking soda

1 teaspoon baking powder

¼ teaspoon salt

½ cup chopped walnuts, cranberries, or dark chocolate chips (optional)

Prep tip: It's important to let the batter rest to give the flour a chance to absorb the liquid. If you skip this step, your muffins will be dense and won't rise properly.

1. Preheat the oven to 350°F. Spray a nonstick muffin pan with nonstick cooking spray.

2. In a large bowl, mash the bananas, then stir in the honey. Beat the egg into the mixture, then add the almond milk, yogurt, and vanilla.

3. In another large bowl, combine the flour, baking soda, baking powder, and salt.

4. Add the flour mixture to the banana mixture and stir until just combined. Be careful not to overmix. Add the walnuts, cranberries, or chocolate chips (if using).

5. Let the batter rest for 20 minutes.

6. Using a ¼-cup scoop, pour batter into each muffin cup.

7. Bake for 15 to 18 minutes or until the muffins are just starting to brown.

8. Let sit for 2 minutes, then remove the muffins from the pan and cool on a cooling rack.

LOW-CARB • SOY-FREE
GLUTEN-FREE: *Substitute any gluten-free flour for the whole-wheat pastry flour.*
NUT-FREE: *Substitute dairy or soy milk for the almond milk.*

Per muffin: Calories: 65; Fat: 1g; Carbs: 14g; Fiber: 1g; Sugar: 9g; Protein: 2g; Sodium: 171mg

Greek Egg White Omelet

SERVES 2

EQUIPMENT: Large nonstick skillet
PREP TIME: 10 minutes
COOK TIME: 10 minutes

You can make an omelet out of all egg whites, but I prefer to use a couple of whole eggs for a fluffy and satisfying texture. Since feta has a strong flavor, you don't need a lot to make this breakfast really tasty.

1 teaspoon olive oil

½ cup loosely packed spinach leaves

¼ cup diced red onion

2 garlic cloves, minced

¼ cup diced tomatoes

2 eggs

4 egg whites

2 tablespoons almond milk

2 tablespoons crumbled feta cheese

1. Heat the olive oil in a large nonstick skillet over medium heat. Add the spinach, onion, and garlic, and cook for 2 to 3 minutes. Add the tomatoes and continue to cook for 2 minutes more, stirring occasionally.

2. In a small bowl, whisk together the eggs, egg whites, and almond milk.

3. Add the egg mixture to the skillet, tilting the pan to coat the spinach mixture with the eggs.

4. Cook for 2 to 3 minutes until the eggs are almost set, stirring gently so the eggs cook evenly and tilting the pan to let the softer parts of the egg mixture flow to the edges to cook.

5. Scatter the cheese over the top, and continue to cook for 1 to 2 minutes until the eggs are set but still moist.

6. Carefully fold the omelet in half, then cut into two pieces and serve.

GLUTEN-FREE • LOW-CARB • SOY-FREE
DAIRY-FREE: *Skip the feta and add a pinch salt, if needed.*

Per serving: Calories: 158; Fat: 9g; Carbs: 5g; Fiber: 1g; Sugar: 3g; Protein: 15g; Sodium: 241mg

Mini Egg Frittatas

SERVES 4
EQUIPMENT: 8- or 12-cup nonstick muffin pan
PREP TIME: 10 minutes
COOK TIME: 25 minutes

These mini egg frittatas are a great low-carb breakfast option, and you can customize the fillings however you like. Swap out the onion and bell pepper for spinach and mushrooms for a different flavor.

Nonstick cooking spray

6 eggs

¼ cup diced yellow onion

¼ cup diced green bell pepper

2 tablespoons almond milk

¼ teaspoon garlic powder

Pinch salt

Pinch freshly ground
black pepper

2 tablespoons shredded
Parmesan cheese (optional)

1. Preheat the oven to 350°F. Spray a nonstick muffin pan with nonstick cooking spray.

2. In a large bowl, whisk together the eggs, onion, bell pepper, almond milk, garlic powder, salt, pepper, and cheese (if using).

3. Pour the egg mixture evenly into 8 muffin cups.

4. Bake for 20 to 22 minutes until the eggs are set.

5. Let sit for 5 minutes before serving.

Flexitarian tip: Add ½ cup cooked ground turkey to the egg mixture before baking.

GLUTEN-FREE • LOW-CARB • SOY-FREE
DAIRY-FREE: *Skip the cheese and add 2 more tablespoons diced bell pepper.*
NUT-FREE: *Substitute soy milk or dairy milk for the almond milk.*

Per serving (2 mini frittatas): Calories: 104; Fat: 7g; Carbs: 2g; Fiber: 0g; Sugar: 1g; Protein: 9g; Sodium: 143mg

Spicy Breakfast Tacos

SERVES 4
EQUIPMENT: Small saucepan, large nonstick skillet
PREP TIME: 15 minutes
COOK TIME: 15 minutes

Why save tacos for dinner? These mildly spicy tacos are great for breakfast or brunch, especially for a group. You can easily double the recipe to feed a crowd, and everyone can customize their taco with their favorite toppings.

1 (15-ounce) can black beans, drained and rinsed

½ teaspoon dried oregano

½ teaspoon ground cumin

½ teaspoon garlic powder

¼ teaspoon chili powder

¼ teaspoon salt, plus pinch

8 eggs

Hot sauce (optional)

Pinch freshly ground black pepper

8 corn tortillas

Nonstick cooking spray

½ cup pico de gallo or tomato salsa

1 avocado, sliced

1. In a small saucepan, heat the black beans over medium heat. Add the oregano, cumin, garlic powder, chili powder, and ¼ teaspoon of salt. Cook for 5 to 7 minutes, stirring occasionally, until heated through.

2. In a large bowl, beat the eggs with the hot sauce (if using). Add the remaining pinch of salt and the pepper.

3. In a large nonstick skillet over medium heat, lightly toast the tortillas until they begin to brown, about 30 seconds on each side. Remove the tortillas and set aside, covered by a kitchen towel.

4. Spray the skillet with nonstick cooking spray. Add the eggs and cook over medium-low heat until lightly set, scraping the pan frequently to keep them scrambled.

5. To assemble, top each tortilla with some of the scrambled eggs, black beans, pico de gallo or salsa, and avocado slices.

6. Sprinkle with more salt, pepper, and hot sauce, if desired.

DAIRY-FREE • GLUTEN-FREE • SOY-FREE

Per serving (2 tacos): Calories: 306; Fat: 12g; Carbs: 32g; Fiber: 7g; Sugar: 2g; Protein: 19g; Sodium: 316mg

Salt-and-Vinegar Brussels Sprout Chips, page 46

CHAPTER 4

Snacks and Sides

I like to keep healthy snacks around when I need a bite between meals. Don't worry, healthy snacks aren't just baby carrots and celery sticks. These snacks are packed with flavor. They are perfect for your next party or event, because they're easy to make and many of them can be made in advance. All of these recipes are full of healthy ingredients, so snack away!

White Bean and Sage Dip

MAKES 2 CUPS [¼ CUP = 1 SERVING]
EQUIPMENT: Medium nonstick skillet, blender or food processor
PREP TIME: 5 minutes
COOK TIME: 5 minutes

This dip might remind you of hummus, but cannellini beans are softer than chickpeas, so the texture is extra creamy. Cooking the sage and garlic in olive oil gives this dip its savory flavor, so don't skip that step. Serve this with vegetables or pita chips at your next party.

¼ cup olive oil

1 teaspoon chopped fresh sage

3 garlic cloves, minced

2 (15-ounce) cans cannellini beans, drained and rinsed

1 tablespoon pine nuts (optional)

Cucumbers and carrots, cut into sticks, or pita chips, for serving

1. Heat the olive oil in a medium nonstick skillet over medium heat for 1 minute. Add the sage and garlic and continue to cook for 2 minutes.

2. Remove from the heat and stir in the cannellini beans.

3. Scrape the mixture into a blender or food processor and blend until slightly chunky.

4. Sprinkle with the pine nuts (if using) just before serving.

5. Serve with cut cucumbers, carrots, and/or pita chips.

DAIRY-FREE • GLUTEN-FREE • LOW-CARB
SOY-FREE • VEGAN

Per ¼-cup serving: Calories: 163; Fat: 7g; Carbs: 19g; Fiber: 7g; Sugar: 2g; Protein: 7g; Sodium: 379mg

The Truly Healthy Vegetarian Cookbook

Black Bean and Corn Salsa

MAKES 3 CUPS [¼ CUP = 1 SERVING]
EQUIPMENT: Large nonstick skillet
PREP TIME: 10 minutes
COOK TIME: 15 minutes

This black bean and corn salsa is a favorite with tortilla chips, but it can be used as so much more than just a dip. It's delicious in tacos and wraps, and it makes a hearty salad topping. I often add a couple of scoops on top of a bowl of chopped romaine lettuce for a quick and easy salad.

1 (15-ounce) can sweet corn, drained and rinsed

1 (15-ounce) can black beans, drained and rinsed

¼ cup diced red onion

1 jalapeño pepper, seeded and diced

Juice of 1 lime

1 teaspoon honey

½ teaspoon salt, plus more if needed

1 avocado, diced

1. In a large nonstick skillet, sauté the corn over medium heat. (You can add a bit of oil to the skillet if you like, but you don't need to.) Cook for 10 to 12 minutes, stirring occasionally, until lightly browned.

2. In a large bowl, combine the cooked corn with the black beans. Stir in the onion and jalapeño pepper.

3. In a small bowl, whisk together the lime juice, honey, and salt.

4. Drizzle the dressing over the bean and corn mixture. Taste and add more salt if needed.

5. Gently stir in the avocado just before serving.

Make-ahead tip: This dish can be made ahead of time, but leave out the avocado. Let all the other flavors blend for up to 6 hours in the refrigerator, then add the avocado just before serving.

DAIRY-FREE • GLUTEN-FREE • LOW-CARB
NUT-FREE • SOY-FREE
VEGAN: *Use agave nectar instead of honey.*

Per ¼-cup serving: Calories: 78; Fat: 4g; Carbs: 11g; Fiber: 3g; Sugar: 2g; Protein: 2g; Sodium: 181mg

Fruit Skewers with Dark Chocolate Yogurt Dip

SERVES 4
EQUIPMENT: Bamboo skewers
PREP TIME: 15 minutes

Warning: You might end up eating this chocolate yogurt dip with a spoon! But don't worry, it's full of good-for-you ingredients. I like to use dark cocoa powder, which you can find at most grocery stores. Not only does it give this a rich, chocolaty taste, cocoa is also a good source of iron.

For the dip

½ cup plain Greek yogurt

2 tablespoons dark cocoa powder

¼ teaspoon pure vanilla extract

1 tablespoon honey

For the fruit skewers

1 cup strawberries, hulled and halved

1 cup peeled, cored, and chopped pineapple (about ¼ medium pineapple)

1 cup pitted and chopped peaches (1 to 2 peaches)

1 cup blackberries

Make-ahead tip: The dip can be made up to 2 days in advance and stored in the refrigerator in an airtight container. But cut the fruit and assemble the skewers just before serving.

TO MAKE THE DIP

Combine the yogurt, cocoa powder, vanilla, and honey. You can simply stir them together in a medium bowl, or, if your cocoa powder is clumpy, you may want to blend the ingredients in a blender for a smoother texture.

TO MAKE THE SKEWERS

1. Thread the chunks of fruit onto bamboo skewers, alternating types of fruit for variety. There should be 6 to 8 pieces of fruit on each skewer.

2. Serve the skewers with a side of the dip to dunk the pieces of fruit in.

GLUTEN-FREE • LOW-CARB • NUT-FREE • SOY-FREE

DAIRY-FREE: *Use coconut milk yogurt or almond milk yogurt in place of the Greek yogurt. If your nondairy yogurt has added sugar, taste the dip before adding the honey; you may not need as much.*

VEGAN: *Go dairy-free, and also replace the honey with agave nectar.*

Per serving: Calories: 99; Fat: 1g; Carbs: 20g; Fiber: 5g; Sugar: 14g; Protein: 5g; Sodium: 14mg

Spicy Edamame

SERVES 4
EQUIPMENT: Large pot, large skillet
PREP TIME: 5 minutes
COOK TIME: 10 minutes

I love serving this edamame as an easy appetizer when we're having a stir-fry for dinner. Edamame isn't just high in protein and fiber, it's also a good source of minerals, including calcium, iron, magnesium, potassium, and zinc. If you're not a fan of spicy foods, you can cut down on the red pepper flakes, but I love the flavor they give this dish.

1 pound frozen edamame still in pods

1 tablespoon olive oil

4 garlic cloves, pressed or minced

¼ teaspoon red pepper flakes

Sea salt

Soy sauce, for serving

1. Bring a large pot of salted water to a boil. Add the edamame and boil for 2 to 3 minutes until bright green and tender.

2. While the edamame cooks, heat the olive oil in a large skillet over medium heat for 30 seconds. Add the garlic and red pepper flakes, and cook over medium heat for 3 to 4 minutes.

3. Drain the edamame and add to the skillet. Stir to coat the edamame with the flavored oil.

4. Transfer to a serving bowl and season with sea salt. Serve with soy sauce on the side for dipping.

Ingredient tip: Edamame is easy to find in the frozen-food section, with or near the vegetables. Look for edamame still in the pods, as some is sold without the pods (shelled). To eat, dip an edamame pod in the sauce, then gently pull the pod through your teeth, removing the beans. Discard the pod.

DAIRY-FREE • LOW-CARB • NUT-FREE • VEGAN

Per serving: Calories: 210; Fat: 11g; Carbs: 16g; Fiber: 5g; Sugar: 0g; Protein: 15g; Sodium: 77mg

Salt-and-Vinegar Brussels Sprout Chips

SERVES 4

EQUIPMENT: Nonstick baking sheet
PREP TIME: 15 minutes
COOK TIME: 20 minutes

Brussels sprout chips might sound weird, but you'll be surprised at how good they are. When the thin leaves of a Brussels sprout are baked, they get super crispy. You want the oven temperature to be low because the goal is not to roast the sprout leaves but to dehydrate them, which makes them crunchy without needing a lot of oil. The white balsamic vinegar gives these a flavor that will remind you of your favorite salt-and-vinegar potato chips.

1 pound Brussels sprouts

1 tablespoon avocado oil

2 tablespoons white balsamic vinegar

¼ teaspoon salt

Prep tip: Peeling apart Brussels sprouts might sound time-consuming, but the larger layers will typically fall off after you trim the ends. Separate the rest of the larger leaves, and when you get to the tightly compacted center, set it aside. Save the small hearts to toss into a salad or stir-fry.

1. Preheat the oven to 250°F.

2. Trim the ends off the Brussels sprouts and peel the layers apart into individual leaves.

3. Combine the avocado oil and vinegar in a large zip-top bag. Add the sprout leaves to the bag and gently toss until evenly coated.

4. Spread the leaves in a single layer on a nonstick baking sheet and bake for 15 to 20 minutes until they're brown and crispy.

5. Sprinkle with the salt.

DAIRY-FREE • GLUTEN-FREE • LOW-CARB
NUT-FREE • SOY-FREE • VEGAN

Per serving: Calories: 81; Fat: 4g; Carbs: 10g; Fiber: 4g; Sugar: 3g; Protein: 4g; Sodium: 176mg

Peanut Butter Granola Bars

MAKES 8 BARS [1 BAR = 1 SERVING]
EQUIPMENT: 9-by-4-inch nonstick loaf pan
PREP TIME: 5 minutes
COOK TIME: 15 minutes

These granola bars are a perfectly portable snack that you can make at the start of the week and grab on your way out the door. If you don't have almond flour, you can grind almonds in a blender or food processor to make your own.

Nonstick cooking spray

⅓ cup honey

½ cup natural crunchy peanut butter

½ cup rolled oats

½ cup almond flour

½ cup sliced almonds

1. Preheat the oven to 350°F. Spray a 9-by-4-inch nonstick loaf pan with nonstick cooking spray.

2. In a large bowl, combine the honey and peanut butter.

3. Stir in the oats, almond flour, and almonds until combined.

4. Press the oat mixture into the bottom of the prepared loaf plan.

5. Bake for 14 to 17 minutes until the edges just begin to brown. It might still be a little soft but will firm up when cool.

6. Make sure to let cool completely in the pan, then cut into 8 bars.

7. Store in an airtight container.

Substitution tip: You can substitute cashew butter or almond butter for the peanut butter if you like.

DAIRY-FREE • GLUTEN-FREE • LOW-CARB • SOY-FREE
VEGAN: *Use agave nectar instead of honey.*

Per bar: Calories: 298; Fat: 20g; Carbs: 25g; Fiber: 4g; Sugar: 15g; Protein: 9g; Sodium: 67mg

Roasted Broccoli with Almonds

SERVES 4
EQUIPMENT: Nonstick baking sheet
PREP TIME: 10 minutes
COOK TIME: 10 minutes

If someone tells you they don't like broccoli, make them this dish. When broccoli is roasted until it's browned and crispy, it's irresistible. I love serving this with a homemade veggie burger or as a side dish with my favorite pasta. To be honest, you could eat this broccoli with just about anything!

1 head broccoli

1 tablespoon olive oil

Juice of 1 lemon

¼ teaspoon salt

Pinch freshly ground black pepper

¼ cup slivered almonds

1. Preheat the oven to 425°F.

2. Cut the broccoli florets into 1-inch pieces, discarding the woody stem.

3. In a large bowl, toss the broccoli with the olive oil, lemon juice, salt, and pepper.

4. Spread the broccoli pieces on a nonstick baking sheet and roast for 8 minutes, then flip the pieces over and sprinkle with the almonds.

5. Roast the broccoli and almonds together for 2 to 3 minutes more, until browned.

DAIRY-FREE • GLUTEN-FREE • LOW-CARB
SOY-FREE • VEGAN

Per serving: Calories: 106; Fat: 7g; Carbs: 9g; Fiber: 4g; Sugar: 2g; Protein: 5g; Sodium: 187mg

Lemon-Parmesan Asparagus

SERVES 4
EQUIPMENT: Large nonstick skillet
PREP TIME: 5 minutes
COOK TIME: 10 minutes

This recipe is one of the quickest and easiest ways to prepare asparagus, and it tastes wonderful, too. Be sure not to overcook the asparagus; it's best with a little bit of crunch. The spears will cook very quickly if they're thin and a bit more slowly if they're thick. Either way, they're done when they are tender-crisp. I love serving this with roasted sweet potatoes and veggie burgers or a simple pasta dish.

1 pound asparagus

1 tablespoon olive oil

Juice of ½ lemon

½ cup shredded Parmesan cheese

Salt

1. Trim the tough ends off the bottom of the asparagus with a sharp knife.

2. Heat the olive oil in a large nonstick skillet over medium heat for 30 seconds. Add the asparagus and cook for 4 minutes.

3. Pour the lemon juice over the asparagus and continue to cook until tender-crisp, 1 to 3 minutes.

4. Remove from the pan and sprinkle with the Parmesan cheese and salt.

Ingredient tip: One cup of asparagus contains just 30 calories and provides 3 grams of protein and 3 grams of fiber, making it one of the healthiest foods you'll find at the grocery store.

GLUTEN-FREE • LOW-CARB • NUT-FREE • SOY-FREE
DAIRY-FREE/VEGAN: *Leave out the cheese and sprinkle with 2 teaspoons nutritional yeast and additional salt to taste.*

Per serving: Calories: 100; Fat: 7g; Carbs: 5g; Fiber: 2g; Sugar: 2g; Protein: 7g; Sodium: 174mg

Ten-Minute Green Beans

When I need a super quick and easy side dish, these green beans come to the rescue. They're salty and spicy, with just enough crunch. They're delicious served with tofu, tempeh, or grilled portobello mushrooms. You'll find sesame oil in the Asian-foods aisle of your supermarket or at an Asian grocery store.

1 tablespoon avocado oil

1 pound green beans

1 tablespoon soy sauce

1 teaspoon sesame oil

¼ teaspoon red pepper flakes

1. Heat the avocado oil in a large nonstick skillet over medium heat for 30 seconds. Add the green beans and cook for 4 minutes, stirring occasionally.

2. Add the soy sauce and continue to cook for about 4 more minutes until lightly browned.

3. Drizzle with the sesame oil and sprinkle with the red pepper flakes just before serving.

Ingredient tip: Sesame oil has a very low smoke point (it burns easily), so it isn't great for stir-frying. But it has a great flavor, which makes it a perfect finishing oil.

DAIRY-FREE • LOW-CARB • NUT-FREE • VEGAN

Per serving: Calories: 79; Fat: 5g; Carbs: 9g; Fiber: 4g; Sugar: 2g; Protein: 2g; Sodium: 232mg

Garlic Sweet Potato Oven Fries

SERVES 4

EQUIPMENT: Nonstick baking sheet
PREP TIME: 10 minutes
COOK TIME: 20 minutes

Veggie burgers served with a side of sweet potato fries are a common dish at our house, especially in the summertime. The only things I love more than crispy sweet potato fries are crispy sweet potato fries topped with garlic. Make sure you roast the sweet potato wedges long enough that they get browned on the outside.

Nonstick cooking spray

2 large sweet potatoes

1 tablespoon olive oil

4 garlic cloves, minced

1 teaspoon salt

1. Preheat the oven to 450°F. Spray a nonstick baking sheet with nonstick cooking spray.

2. Peel the sweet potatoes and cut them into wedges.

3. In a large bowl, toss the potato wedges with the olive oil. Spread them evenly on the prepared baking sheet.

4. Roast for 10 minutes, flip, and continue to roast for 10 minutes more or until browned on both sides.

5. Sprinkle with the garlic and salt before serving.

Prep tip: As much as possible, cut the sweet potatoes into uniform wedges. That will ensure that you're able to get them nicely browned without burning any or leaving some undercooked.

DAIRY-FREE • GLUTEN-FREE • NUT-FREE
SOY-FREE • VEGAN

Per serving: Calories: 101; Fat: 4g; Carbs: 12g; Fiber: 2g; Sugar: 4g; Protein: 1g; Sodium: 604mg

Spicy Zucchini Oven Fries

SERVES 4
EQUIPMENT: Nonstick baking sheet
PREP TIME: 15 minutes
COOK TIME: 20 minutes

The bread crumbs and cayenne pepper give these zucchini fries a crunchy texture with a spicy kick! I like eating mine with a side of ketchup. Pair them with Spicy Black Bean Burgers (page 97).

Nonstick cooking spray

⅔ cup whole-wheat bread crumbs

½ teaspoon salt

2 teaspoons garlic powder

¼ teaspoon cayenne pepper (or to taste)

½ teaspoon chili powder

1½ pounds (about 3 small) zucchini

1 egg, beaten

1. Preheat the oven to 425°F. Spray a nonstick baking sheet with nonstick cooking spray.

2. In a small bowl, mix together the bread crumbs, salt, garlic powder, cayenne pepper, and chili powder, then spread the mixture on a plate.

3. Cut the zucchini into thin sticks about 3 inches long (the shape of a typical french fry).

4. Pour the beaten egg into a large bowl and add the zucchini, lightly tossing to coat.

5. Roll the zucchini sticks in the bread crumbs until they're coated on all sides. You may need to do this in batches.

6. Arrange the breaded zucchini in a single layer on the prepared baking sheet. Roast on the center rack for 10 minutes.

7. Turn the zucchini fries over. Continue to roast until golden and just tender, 8 to 10 minutes more.

Ingredient tip: If you don't have any bread crumbs on hand, you can make your own by simply toasting a slice of whole-wheat bread and blending it in a food processor until crumbled.

DAIRY-FREE • LOW-CARB • NUT-FREE • SOY-FREE

Per serving: Calories: 69; Fat: 2g; Carbs: 10g; Fiber: 3g; Sugar: 4g; Protein: 4g; Sodium: 291mg

Strawberry and Goat Cheese Salad, page 56

CHAPTER 5

Substantial Salads

Salads might have a reputation for being "diet food" (or even "rabbit food"), but I'm here to tell you that salads deserve to be reconsidered. The trick to making them satisfying and delicious is to use a mix of carbohydrates, protein, and healthy fats. I also like salads with lots of texture, so crunchy toppings and hearty greens are a must. Once you try these salads, you won't leave them for the rabbits.

Strawberry and Goat Cheese Salad

This strawberry and goat cheese salad is lovely in the summertime when strawberries are plump and sweet. Three tablespoons of shelled hemp seeds contain more than 10 grams of protein, which helps make this salad super satisfying. For a different twist, replace the dressing here with Sweet Poppy Seed Dressing (page 19).

2 tablespoons honey

⅓ cup olive oil

3 tablespoons balsamic vinegar

¼ teaspoon paprika

¼ teaspoon salt

4 cups strawberries, hulled

8 cups fresh spinach or mixed greens

4 ounces goat cheese, crumbled

½ cup chopped walnuts

½ cup shelled hemp seeds or 1 cup cooked quinoa

1. In a medium bowl, whisk together the honey, olive oil, vinegar, paprika, and salt. Set the dressing aside and let the flavors blend for at least 10 minutes.

2. Thinly slice the strawberries.

3. In a large bowl, top the spinach with the strawberries, goat cheese, walnuts, and hemp seeds or quinoa.

4. Toss with the dressing just before serving.

Flexitarian tip: Swap the hemp seeds or quinoa for 1 cup chopped grilled chicken.

GLUTEN-FREE • LOW-CARB • SOY-FREE
DAIRY-FREE: *Skip the goat cheese and add 1 avocado, diced.*
VEGAN: *Go dairy-free, and substitute agave nectar for the honey.*

Per serving: Calories: 560; Fat: 43g; Carbs: 38g; Fiber: 7g; Sugar: 21g; Protein: 12g; Sodium: 305mg

Kale, Apple, and Walnut Salad

SERVES 4

PREP TIME: 15 minutes

This is one of my favorite salads to make in the fall. The sweet apples and cranberries are delicious with the crunchy walnuts. Most apples work fine in this salad, but I recommend something red, sweet, and crisp, like Fuji, Gala, or Honeycrisp. Massaging the kale breaks down the dense, chewy fibers, which makes it much easier to eat.

2 bunches kale

2 tablespoons freshly squeezed lemon juice

¼ cup olive oil

Pinch salt

2 large red apples, cored and chopped

½ cup walnut pieces

¼ cup dried cranberries

1. De-stem the kale by pulling the leaves off the tough center stems. Tear the leaves into smaller pieces and place in a large bowl.

2. In a small bowl, whisk together the lemon juice, olive oil, and salt. Drizzle the dressing over the kale. Using your hands, massage the kale leaves with the dressing for about 1 minute.

3. Add the chopped apple, walnuts, and cranberries, and serve.

Flexitarian tip: Reduce the walnuts to 2 tablespoons and add 1 cup sliced grilled chicken breast.

DAIRY-FREE • GLUTEN-FREE • SOY-FREE • VEGAN

NUT-FREE: *Leave out the walnuts and add shelled pumpkin seeds.*

Per serving: Calories: 340; Fat: 23g; Carbs: 34g; Fiber: 6g; Sugar: 14g; Protein: 7g; Sodium: 100mg

Shaved Brussels Sprouts and Pine Nuts Salad

SERVES 4
EQUIPMENT: Mandoline or food processor
PREP TIME: 15 minutes

I love chopped salads with a crunchy texture, and this Brussels sprouts salad is one of my favorites. When making a salad with just a few components, like this one, it's critical to use high-quality ingredients. Grate fresh Parmesan and use a high-quality olive oil; their superior flavor will be noticeable.

2 pounds Brussels sprouts

¼ cup olive oil

¼ cup freshly squeezed lemon juice (from about 2 lemons)

4 ounces Parmesan cheese, finely grated

¼ cup pine nuts

Salt

Freshly ground black pepper

1. Using a sharp knife, trim the ends off the Brussels sprouts. Discard the ends and the outermost layer of leaves.

2. Using a mandoline, thinly slice the Brussels sprouts, or shred them using a food processor fitted with a shredding disc. Place the sprouts in a large mixing bowl.

3. In a small dish, combine the olive oil and lemon juice.

4. Add the dressing to the shaved Brussels sprouts and toss to coat.

5. Sprinkle with the Parmesan cheese and pine nuts, and season with salt and pepper.

Prep tip: If you don't have a mandoline or a food processor, a sharp knife will also do the trick.

GLUTEN-FREE • LOW-CARB • SOY-FREE
DAIRY-FREE/VEGAN: *Leave out the cheese, and add 1 more tablespoon olive oil and ¼ cup salted sunflower seeds.*

Per serving: Calories: 358; Fat: 27g; Carbs: 23g; Fiber: 9g; Sugar: 6g; Protein: 18g; Sodium: 362mg

Tomato, Cucumber, and Chickpea Salad

SERVES 4

PREP TIME: 15 minutes

If you love Greek salads, you must try this chopped salad. It might seem strange having a salad without any lettuce or other greens, but it's packed with so many vegetables, you won't even notice. Try it with falafel on top, like the ones in the Spinach Falafel Wraps (page 92).

1 pound tomatoes

2 medium cucumbers

2 (15-ounce) cans chickpeas, drained and rinsed

¼ cup crumbled feta cheese

¼ cup chopped fresh dill

2 tablespoons olive oil

2 teaspoons balsamic vinegar

Salt

Freshly ground black pepper

1. Cut the tomatoes into large chunks.

2. Cut the cucumber into thick slices, then cut the slices into quarters.

3. Combine the tomatoes, cucumbers, and chickpeas in a large bowl.

4. Sprinkle with the feta and dill.

5. Drizzle with the olive oil and vinegar, and season with salt and pepper.

Ingredient tip: Make this salad when tomatoes are in season. They're the backbone of this dish, so you want them bursting with flavor.

GLUTEN-FREE • NUT-FREE • SOY-FREE

DAIRY-FREE/VEGAN: *Leave out the feta and substitute ¼ cup salted pine nuts.*

Per serving: Calories: 421; Fat: 12g; Carbs: 66g; Fiber: 13g; Sugar: 6g; Protein: 16g; Sodium: 876mg

Black Bean and Avocado Salad

This black bean and avocado salad is like a vegan taco in a bowl. Make sure your avocados are ripe, as their flavor and texture are important in this dish. You can add a pinch of chili powder if you like a spicier flavor, although the jalapeño pepper is usually hot enough for most.

2 (15-ounce) cans black beans, drained and rinsed

2 orange bell peppers, seeded and cut into thin strips

1 jalapeño pepper, halved and seeded

½ cup roughly chopped fresh cilantro

½ teaspoon ground cumin

2 tablespoons freshly squeezed lime juice

2 tablespoons olive oil

Pinch salt, plus more if needed

2 avocados, diced

1. In a large bowl, combine the black beans, bell peppers, and jalapeño pepper, and toss gently. Stir in the cilantro.

2. In a small bowl, whisk together the cumin, lime juice, olive oil, and salt.

3. Drizzle the dressing over the salad.

4. Add the avocados just before serving.

5. Check the seasoning and add more salt if necessary.

Prep tip: When chopping jalapeño peppers, you may want to wear gloves. Capsaicin, the spicy component of the pepper, can burn your skin.

DAIRY-FREE • GLUTEN-FREE • NUT-FREE
SOY-FREE • VEGAN

Per serving: Calories: 399; Fat: 28g; Carbs: 34g; Fiber: 15g; Sugar: 5g; Protein: 10g; Sodium: 58mg

Chopped Taco Salad

SERVES 4
EQUIPMENT: Large nonstick skillet
PREP TIME: 20 minutes, plus 1 hour to marinate
COOK TIME: 10 minutes

I love chopped salads because each bite is so full of flavor. In this one, chopping the cilantro and tossing it with the romaine helps add flavor without requiring additional salad dressing. The tempeh ends up resembling the ground meat of a traditional taco and makes this salad extra filling. You can find tempeh in the refrigerated case in the natural-foods section of your supermarket or in a health food store. It's usually sold next to the tofu. Many versions come flavored, so be sure to get plain tempeh for this recipe.

1 (8-ounce) package tempeh

3 tablespoons soy sauce

1 tablespoon maple syrup

1 garlic clove, minced

2 teaspoons avocado oil

6 cups chopped romaine lettuce

1 cup chopped fresh cilantro

1 (15-ounce) can black beans, drained and rinsed

1 red bell pepper, seeded and diced

½ cup corn kernels, canned or fresh

½ pound fresh tomatoes, diced

½ cup Avocado Ranch Dressing (page 20)

1. Cut the tempeh into thin strips.

2. In a medium bowl, whisk together the soy sauce, maple syrup, and garlic. Add the tempeh and toss to coat. Marinate for at least 1 hour.

3. In a large nonstick skillet, heat the avocado oil over medium heat. Add the marinated tempeh to the skillet in a single layer and cook for 5 to 7 minutes until browned on one side. Flip and continue to cook for 3 to 4 minutes more until browned and crispy. Transfer to a paper towel and set aside to cool.

4. Once cooled, crumble the tempeh strips into small pieces.

CONTINUED

5. In a large bowl, toss the romaine lettuce and cilantro. Top with the tempeh crumbles, black beans, bell pepper, corn, and tomatoes.

6. Drizzle with the Avocado Ranch Dressing and serve immediately.

Make-ahead tip: The tempeh can be cooked up to 2 days in advance. Store in an airtight container in the refrigerator.

NUT-FREE
DAIRY-FREE/VEGAN: *Skip the Avocado Ranch Dressing. Instead, mash 1 avocado with 2 tablespoons olive oil, 1 table-spoon lime juice, and a pinch each of salt and pepper. Thin with water if desired, and use this mixture as the dressing.*

Per serving: Calories: 403; Fat: 18g; Carbs: 45g; Fiber: 12g; Sugar: 9g; Protein: 23g; Sodium: 835mg

Three-Bean Salad

SERVES 6
EQUIPMENT: Large pot
PREP TIME: 15 minutes
COOK TIME: 5 minutes

This three-bean salad is a classic picnic dish. You can eat it by itself or on top of a bed of your favorite greens. It can be prepared ahead of time and served cold or at room temperature. The beans make this salad particularly filling.

1 pound green beans

2 (15-ounce) cans low-sodium kidney beans, drained and rinsed

2 (15-ounce) cans low-sodium chickpeas, drained and rinsed

¼ cup olive oil

2 tablespoons balsamic vinegar

1 teaspoon honey

¼ teaspoon garlic powder

½ teaspoon salt

Pinch freshly ground black pepper

½ cup sliced almonds

1. Fill a large bowl with ice water.

2. Bring a large pot of water to a boil. Add the green beans and cook for 3 to 4 minutes until bright green. Remove them with a slotted spoon and immediately transfer to the ice water. Set aside until they are cool to the touch. Once cooled, cut them into 1½-inch pieces.

3. In a large bowl, combine the green beans with the kidney beans and chickpeas.

4. In a small bowl, whisk together the olive oil, vinegar, honey, garlic powder, salt, and pepper.

5. Drizzle the dressing over the beans and toss to coat. Sprinkle with the almonds.

Make-ahead tip: This salad can be made a day in advance. Keep it in an airtight container in the refrigerator.

DAIRY-FREE • GLUTEN-FREE • SOY-FREE
VEGAN: *Substitute agave nectar for the honey.*

Per serving: Calories: 480; Fat: 15g; Carbs: 71g; Fiber: 20g; Sugar: 6g; Protein: 20g; Sodium: 307mg

Warm Kale with Chickpeas and Sweet Potato

SERVES 4
EQUIPMENT: Nonstick baking sheet, large nonstick skillet
PREP TIME: 15 minutes
COOK TIME: 45 minutes

Warm salad might sound a little strange, but it's a delicious way to enjoy kale. Cooked kale is easier to digest than raw, so if you're not used to eating this high-fiber superfood, I suggest starting out with this warm salad. When heated, this hearty green wilts slightly but still maintains some structure. The sweet potatoes make this salad extra satisfying, and the Roasted Chickpeas (page 26) are almost like crunchy croutons.

2 medium sweet potatoes, peeled and cut into 1-inch pieces

2 (15-ounce) cans chickpeas, drained and rinsed

3 tablespoons olive oil, divided

2 teaspoons herbes de Provence

2 teaspoons honey

2 teaspoons apple cider vinegar

2 bunches curly kale

1. Preheat the oven to 425°F.

2. Spread the sweet potatoes and chickpeas on a nonstick baking sheet and toss with 2 tablespoons of olive oil and the herbes de Provence.

3. Roast for 40 minutes, turning once after 20 minutes, until the sweet potatoes and chickpeas are brown and crispy.

4. In a small bowl, whisk together the honey, the remaining 1 tablespoon of olive oil, and the vinegar. Set aside.

5. De-stem the kale by pulling the leaves off the tough stems. Discard the stems and tear the leaves into 2-inch pieces. Place in a large nonstick skillet. Pour the dressing over the kale and massage for about 1 minute.

6. Cook over low-medium heat for 3 minutes, stirring frequently, until the kale is bright green and softened. Don't overcook; you want it to be soft but not mushy. You may need to cook the kale in two batches, depending on how large your skillet is.

7. Top the warm kale with the roasted sweet potatoes and chickpeas.

Ingredient tip: Herbes de Provence is a savory dried herb blend that can be found with the spices at most grocery stores.

DAIRY-FREE • GLUTEN-FREE • SOY-FREE

VEGAN: *Substitute agave nectar for the honey.*

Per serving: Calories: 459; Fat: 13g; Carbs: 74g; Fiber: 13g; Sugar: 6g; Protein: 14g; Sodium: 807mg

Hearty Lentil Salad

SERVES 4
EQUIPMENT: Large pot
PREP TIME: 20 minutes
COOK TIME: 30 minutes

I like using French green lentils (also called *puy* lentils) because they hold their shape after cooking, which makes them a great option for a salad. They're often found in the bulk bins at the grocery store, and look almost black before they're cooked. If you can't find them, you can substitute regular green or brown lentils, although the texture will be softer. Manchego cheese is a Spanish sheep's milk cheese. It can be found at most grocery stores with the "gourmet" cheeses. You can substitute Asiago or Pecorino Romano, if you like.

1 cup French green (*puy*) lentils, rinsed and picked over

1 bay leaf

2½ cups water

1 English cucumber

8 ounces cherry tomatoes

2 tablespoons champagne vinegar

2 teaspoons olive oil

2 ounces Manchego cheese

Salt

Substitution tip: You can substitute a regular cucumber for an English cucumber, but cut it into quarters rather than half-moon pieces.

1. Put the lentils and bay leaf in a large pot and cover with the water.

2. Bring to a boil, then lower the heat and simmer for 20 to 30 minutes until the water is absorbed and the lentils are soft but not mushy. Set aside to cool.

3. Halve the cucumber lengthwise, then cut into ¼-inch-thick pieces.

4. Cut the cherry tomatoes in half.

5. In a large bowl, combine the cooled lentils, cucumber, and tomatoes.

6. Drizzle with the vinegar and olive oil. Using a vegetable peeler, shave the Manchego cheese on top of the salad. Season with salt.

GLUTEN-FREE • LOW-CARB • NUT-FREE • SOY-FREE
DAIRY-FREE/VEGAN: *Skip the cheese and toss in ¼ cup sliced almonds and an additional pinch salt.*

Per serving: Calories: 263; Fat: 7g; Carbs: 34g; Fiber: 16g; Sugar: 4g; Protein: 17g; Sodium: 218mg

Avocado, Orange, and Quinoa Salad

SERVES 4

PREP TIME: 15 minutes

The oranges do double duty in this dish, with the reserved juice used to sweeten the dressing and the segments adding a juicy bite to the salad. The creamy avocado slices make this salad extra appetizing. It's light enough to serve as an easy side but satisfying enough for a main. It's important to use ripe avocados, as unripe avocados lack the flavor and texture needed for this salad.

2 navel oranges

¼ cup olive oil

¼ teaspoon salt

Pinch freshly ground black pepper

8 cups mixed greens or spinach

2 avocados, diced

¼ cup sliced almonds

1 cup cooked quinoa, cooled

1. Segment the oranges: Slice off the top, bottom, and peel of each. Over a medium bowl, cut into each orange between the membranes to remove the segments of flesh. Set aside the orange segments.

2. Squeeze what remains of the oranges to release the rest of their juice into the bowl. You should end up with about 3 tablespoons of juice.

3. Whisk the olive oil with the orange juice, and add the salt and pepper. Set aside.

4. Place the mixed greens in a large bowl. Add the avocados. Top with the orange segments, almonds, and quinoa.

5. Toss with the dressing just before serving.

Ingredient tip: To determine if an avocado is ripe, squeeze it gently; it should give just slightly. To ripen an avocado at home, place it in a brown paper bag. This will help concentrate the ethylene gas to encourage it to ripen faster.

DAIRY-FREE • GLUTEN-FREE • SOY-FREE • VEGAN

Per serving: Calories: 410; Fat: 31g; Carbs: 32g; Fiber: 11g; Sugar: 7g; Protein: 8g; Sodium: 203mg

Thai Quinoa Salad

SERVES 4
PREP TIME: 15 minutes

This salad packs a double punch of protein thanks to the quinoa and edamame. If you don't have one of the vegetables on hand, you can substitute bell pepper or cucumber. The key to this delicious salad is using peanut sauce as the dressing.

8 cups mixed greens

2 cups cooked quinoa

½ cup shredded purple cabbage

½ cup shredded carrots

1 cup shelled edamame

¼ cup chopped fresh cilantro

¼ cup chopped cashews

¼ cup Spicy Peanut Sauce (page 21)

1. In a large bowl, toss the greens with the quinoa.

2. Top with the cabbage, carrots, edamame, cilantro, and cashews.

3. Drizzle with the Spicy Peanut Sauce just before serving.

Ingredient tip: I often buy shelled edamame in the freezer section. Simply thaw before using.

DAIRY-FREE • GLUTEN-FREE • VEGAN

Per serving: Calories: 317; Fat: 10g; Carbs: 46g; Fiber: 7g; Sugar: 13g; Protein: 14g; Sodium: 631mg

Garlicky Kale and Quinoa Salad

SERVES 4
EQUIPMENT: Large pot
PREP TIME: 40 minutes
COOK TIME: 15 minutes

One summer, I ate a version of this salad on repeat nearly every day. It's so easy to prepare a big batch of quinoa and salad dressing and enjoy this throughout the week. Kale is a hearty green, so it can stand up to a thick and creamy dressing.

2 cups quinoa

2 cups low-sodium vegetable broth

2 bunches kale

½ cup Garlic-Almond Dressing (page 18)

¼ cup sliced almonds

¼ cup hemp seeds (optional)

1. Rinse the quinoa in cold water, then put in a large pot. Toast the quinoa over medium heat, just until it begins to dry.

2. Add the vegetable broth and bring to a boil. Simmer for about 12 minutes or until all of the broth has been absorbed. Set aside to cool.

3. Tear the kale into pieces, discarding the tough central stems. Place in a large bowl and add the Garlic-Almond Dressing. Massage the kale and dressing for about 1 minute.

4. Let sit for 30 minutes to let the kale soften.

5. Add the cooked quinoa, almonds, and hemp seeds (if using) and mix thoroughly.

Substitution tip: Hemp seeds are a great source of protein, but feel free to substitute additional quinoa or sliced almonds instead.

DAIRY-FREE • GLUTEN-FREE • SOY-FREE • VEGAN

Per serving: Calories: 476; Fat: 14g; Carbs: 72g; Fiber: 9g; Sugar: 1g; Protein: 17g; Sodium: 489mg

Asparagus and Farro Salad

SERVES 4
EQUIPMENT: Large pot
PREP TIME: 20 minutes
COOK TIME: 30 minutes

If you haven't had farro before, I encourage you to try it in this salad. It's a variety of wheat similar to brown rice but with a chewier texture and a nuttier flavor. It's also a good source of fiber, so this salad is guaranteed to fill you up.

1 cup farro

1 pound asparagus, ends trimmed

1 large lemon

2 tablespoons olive oil

½ teaspoon salt

½ teaspoon freshly ground black pepper

½ cup sliced almonds

⅓ cup grated Pecorino Romano cheese

Make-ahead tip: The farro in this recipe can be prepared a day in advance. Keep it in an airtight container in the refrigerator.

1. Rinse the farro and cook according to the package directions.

2. Fill a large bowl with ice water.

3. Bring a large pot of water to a boil. Add the asparagus and cook for 2 to 3 minutes, depending on the thickness of the asparagus. Do not overcook. Drain the asparagus and immediately transfer it to the ice water bath to stop the cooking process.

4. Over a large bowl, zest and juice the lemon. Whisk in the olive oil, salt, and pepper. Set aside.

5. When the farro is done cooking, drain and rinse it in a colander.

6. Transfer the cooled asparagus to a cutting board and cut it into 1-inch pieces.

7. Add the farro and asparagus to the lemon dressing and toss to coat. Top with the almonds and grated cheese.

SOY-FREE

DAIRY-FREE/VEGAN: *Skip the cheese and add an additional ¼ cup sliced almonds and a pinch salt.*

Per serving: Calories: 212; Fat: 6g; Carbs: 33g; Fiber: 4g; Sugar: 3g; Protein: 7g; Sodium: 158mg

Wild Rice Pilaf with Butternut Squash

SERVES 4

EQUIPMENT: Nonstick baking sheet
PREP TIME: 15 minutes
COOK TIME: 30 minutes

This wild rice salad is perfect in the fall, when butternut squash seems to be everywhere. It's delicious with the crunchy almonds and sweet cranberries. I like roasting the squash and onion until they're wonderfully caramelized. This salad can be made up to a day in advance and is delicious served warm, cold, or at room temperature.

Nonstick cooking spray

1 cup wild rice blend

1 butternut squash, peeled, seeded, and cut into 1-inch pieces (3 cups)

1 yellow onion, sliced

1 tablespoon red wine vinegar

2 teaspoons honey

¼ cup slivered almonds

¼ cup dried cranberries

Salt

Freshly ground black pepper

Ingredient tip: Wild rice can be hard to find, but most grocery stores sell a blend of brown rice and wild rice, which works well in this recipe. Feel free to use all wild rice if you're able to find it.

1. Preheat the oven to 400°F. Spray a baking sheet with nonstick cooking spray.

2. Cook the rice according to the package directions.

3. Spread the butternut squash and onion in a single layer on the prepared baking sheet. Roast for 10 minutes. Flip, then continue to roast for 10 more minutes until soft.

4. Transfer the cooked squash, onion, and rice to a large bowl.

5. In a small bowl, whisk together the vinegar and honey.

6. Pour the dressing over the vegetables and rice and toss to coat. Stir in the almonds and cranberries.

7. Season with salt and pepper.

DAIRY-FREE • GLUTEN-FREE • SOY-FREE
VEGAN: *Substitute agave nectar or maple syrup for the honey.*

Per serving: Calories: 279; Fat: 4g; Carbs: 56g; Fiber: 7g; Sugar: 9g; Protein: 7g; Sodium: 44mg

Mediterranean Wheat-Berry Salad

SERVES 4
EQUIPMENT: Large pot
PREP TIME: 15 minutes
COOK TIME: 1 hour

Wheat berries contain the bran, germ, and endosperm of the wheat kernel, which means they're loaded with nutrients. They have a chewy texture and a slightly sweet and nutty flavor. This salad is very dense, so to lighten it up, serve it on top of a bed of mixed greens.

1 cup wheat berries

6 cups water

2 large tomatoes, chopped

1 orange bell pepper, seeded and chopped

¼ cup feta cheese, crumbled

¾ teaspoon dried dill

¼ teaspoon salt

1. Combine the wheat berries and water in a large pot.

2. Bring to a boil, then simmer for 1 hour or until all the water has been absorbed and the wheat berries are tender.

3. Let the wheat berries cool, then transfer them to a large bowl.

4. Toss with the tomatoes, bell pepper, feta, dill, and salt.

NUT-FREE • SOY-FREE
DAIRY-FREE/VEGAN: *Skip the feta and drizzle with 2 tablespoons olive oil and add a pinch salt.*

Per serving: Calories: 220; Fat: 3g; Carbs: 39g; Fiber: 7g; Sugar: 4g; Protein: 10g; Sodium: 259mg

Quinoa Tabbouleh

SERVES 4

EQUIPMENT: Medium pot
PREP TIME: 10 minutes
COOK TIME: 20 minutes

Tabbouleh is traditionally made with bulgur, but quinoa is a nice alternative because it has a little more fiber—plus, you probably already have it in your pantry. This quinoa tabbouleh is wonderful as a salad on its own, but it's delicious in a wrap, too, like the Collard Green Wraps (page 23). Or try it on the Whole-Wheat Flatbreads (page 27) or 100 percent whole-wheat wraps with hummus or tzatziki.

1 cup quinoa

½ cup roughly chopped parsley

1 cucumber, chopped

2 large tomatoes, chopped

1 tablespoon olive oil

¼ teaspoon salt

1. In a medium pot, cook the quinoa according to the package directions and set it aside to cool.

2. In a large bowl, toss the parsley, cucumber, and tomatoes with the olive oil. Sprinkle with the salt.

3. Add the quinoa and stir until combined.

Make-ahead tip: This quinoa tabbouleh can be made up to 1 day in advance. Store in an airtight container in the refrigerator.

DAIRY-FREE • GLUTEN-FREE • NUT-FREE
SOY-FREE • VEGAN

Per serving: Calories: 212; Fat: 6g; Carbs: 33g; Fiber: 4g; Sugar: 3g; Protein: 7g; Sodium: 158mg

Minestrone Soup, page 84

CHAPTER 6

Soups and Stews

Soups and stews are an easy way to eat more vegetables, and these dishes will definitely fill you up. These recipes might require a bit of simmering, but their preparation is quick and many of them can easily be doubled and frozen for later. Broth-based soups with beans or lentils freeze well—just let the soup cool, then transfer to a freezer bag or airtight container. Soups with dairy or pasta shouldn't be frozen.

Hearty Tomato Soup

SERVES 4
EQUIPMENT: Large pot; blender or immersion blender
PREP TIME: 20 minutes
COOK TIME: 10 minutes

You'd never guess the secret to this hearty tomato soup is whole-wheat bread. Blending a few slices of bread into the soup gives it an amazingly velvety texture without any added cream. Make sure you look for whole-wheat bread that doesn't have added sugar and has at least 2 grams of fiber and 3 grams of protein.

8 slices whole-wheat bread

¼ tablespoon olive oil

2 medium yellow onions, chopped

6 garlic cloves, minced

2 (28-ounce) cans whole tomatoes

4 cups low-sodium vegetable broth

Salt

Freshly ground black pepper

Prep tip: Be careful when blending hot soup. If your blender lid has a removable insert in the center, take it out to allow steam to escape.

1. Cut off and discard the bread crusts. Cut the bread into 1-inch-square pieces and set aside.

2. In a large pot, heat the olive oil over medium heat until it is shimmering. Add the onions and garlic and cook for 5 to 6 minutes, stirring frequently, until the onions are translucent.

3. Stir in the tomatoes with their juice. Using a wooden spoon or potato masher, gently break the tomatoes apart until there are no large pieces.

4. Stir in the bread pieces. Raise the heat and bring to a boil, then reduce the heat to medium and cook for 5 more minutes.

5. Let cool slightly, then carefully transfer the mixture to a blender, or use an immersion blender, and blend until smooth, 2 to 3 minutes.

6. Return the soup to the pot and stir in the vegetable broth. Bring the soup to a boil, then season with salt and pepper.

7. Let cool slightly before serving.

DAIRY-FREE · NUT-FREE · SOY-FREE · VEGAN

Per serving: Calories: 385; Fat: 17g; Carbs: 46g; Fiber: 10g; Sugar: 17g; Protein: 17g; Sodium: 173mg

Split Pea Soup

SERVES 4

EQUIPMENT: Large pot; immersion blender, blender, or food processor
PREP TIME: 10 minutes
COOK TIME: 40 minutes

This velvety split pea soup is thick and hearty. You can find split peas at most grocery stores with the dried beans and lentils. This is a great recipe to double and then freeze the leftovers. I love serving this with a small salad or a crusty slice of bread.

1 tablespoon olive oil

1 medium white onion, diced

3 garlic cloves, minced

½ teaspoon dried oregano

8 cups low-sodium vegetable stock

⅓ cup chopped carrots

2 cups dried split peas

Salt

Freshly ground black pepper

1. In a large pot, heat the olive oil over medium heat for 1 minute.

2. Add the onion, garlic, and oregano, and cook until the onion starts getting soft and translucent, about 5 to 6 minutes. Stir frequently so the onion and garlic don't brown.

3. Add the vegetable stock, carrots, and split peas. Bring to a boil, then reduce the heat to low and let simmer for 30 minutes or until the peas are soft.

4. Using an immersion blender, blend the soup until it's just slightly chunky. If you don't have an immersion blender, let the soup cool slightly, then transfer to a blender or food processor and blend until just slightly chunky.

5. Season with salt and pepper.

Ingredient tip: Split peas are a great source of protein, fiber, and folate, making them a nutritional powerhouse.

DAIRY-FREE • GLUTEN-FREE • NUT-FREE
SOY-FREE • VEGAN

Per serving: Calories: 459; Fat: 9g; Carbs: 82g; Fiber: 10g; Sugar: 6g; Protein: 29g; Sodium: 219mg

Cuban Black Bean Soup

SERVES 4
EQUIPMENT: Large pot, immersion blender, blender, or food processor
PREP TIME: 15 minutes
COOK TIME: 25 minutes

The trick to making this soup extra satisfying is to blend half the beans, which creates a hearty base. Keeping the rest of the beans intact makes this feel like a filling stew. If you like, add a little avocado, Greek yogurt, or cilantro on top when serving. This is a great recipe to make ahead of time and reheat for lunch or leftovers.

2 teaspoons olive oil

1 large yellow onion, diced

1 green bell pepper, seeded and diced

6 garlic cloves, minced

1 bay leaf

1 teaspoon ground cumin

4 cups low-sodium vegetable broth

2 (15-ounce) cans black beans, divided

1. In a large pot, heat the olive oil over medium heat for 30 seconds. Add the onion, bell pepper, and garlic, and cook for 5 minutes, stirring occasionally.

2. Add the bay leaf, cumin, vegetable broth, and 1 can of black beans with their liquid.

3. Simmer for 10 minutes, then remove the bay leaf.

4. Using an immersion blender, blend the soup until it's just slightly chunky. If you don't have an immersion blender, let the soup cool slightly, then transfer 3 cups to a blender or food processor and blend until slightly chunky. Transfer the soup back to the pot.

5. Add the remaining can of beans with their liquid, and continue to simmer for 10 minutes.

Ingredient tip: Canned beans often contain a lot of sodium, so I like to use unsalted beans and adjust the salt to taste. This also makes it easier to control the flavor of the dish.

DAIRY-FREE • GLUTEN-FREE • LOW-CARB
NUT-FREE • SOY-FREE • VEGAN

Per serving: Calories: 200; Fat: 5g; Carbs: 27g; Fiber: 9g; Sugar: 4g; Protein: 13g; Sodium: 778mg

Moroccan Cauliflower and Chickpea Soup

SERVES 4

EQUIPMENT: Large pot
PREP TIME: 15 minutes
COOK TIME: 35 minutes

This recipe uses a lot of ingredients you probably already have in your pantry, but it creates a unique blend of flavors. The cauliflower helps add body without a lot of carbohydrates, and the spices give this soup a bright and slightly sweet flavor.

2 teaspoons olive oil

1 yellow onion, diced

2 garlic cloves, minced

½ head cauliflower, cut into 1-inch pieces (about 4 cups)

½ teaspoon paprika

½ teaspoon ground ginger

½ teaspoon salt

1 (15-ounce) can fire-roasted tomatoes

2 (15-ounce) cans sodium-free chickpeas, drained and rinsed

4 cups low-sodium vegetable broth

1. Heat the olive oil in a large pot over medium-low heat. Add the onion and cook for 8 to 10 minutes, stirring occasionally.

2. When the onion is translucent, add the garlic, cauliflower, paprika, ginger, and salt. Raise the heat to medium and cook for 3 minutes, stirring.

3. Add the tomatoes, chickpeas, and broth, and continue to cook for 20 minutes or until the cauliflower is soft.

Ingredient tip: Some fire-roasted tomatoes contain sugar or artificial flavors, so look for organic fire-roasted tomatoes without these extra ingredients. This can be the case with canned beans, too; be sure to check the label.

DAIRY-FREE • GLUTEN-FREE • NUT-FREE
SOY-FREE • VEGAN

Per serving: Calories: 396; Fat: 7g; Carbs: 67g; Fiber: 14g; Sugar: 7g; Protein: 20g; Sodium: 287mg

Spicy Enchilada Soup

This soup contains all the best flavors of enchiladas in a bowl. In my house, we like topping ours with avocado slices and a few crushed tortilla chips, but you can customize it any way you like. If your soup ends up being too spicy, you can cool it down with a splash of milk or a dollop of Greek yogurt on top.

1 tablespoon olive oil

1 medium yellow onion, diced

4 garlic cloves, minced

1½ cups Enchilada Sauce (page 22)

2 (10-ounce) cans sodium-free diced tomatoes with green chilies

1 (14.5-ounce) can sodium-free diced tomatoes

2 (15-ounce) cans sodium-free black beans, drained and rinsed

1 (15-ounce) can sodium-free sweet corn

Juice of 1 lime

1. In a large pot, heat the olive oil for 30 seconds over medium heat. Add the onion and garlic and cook for 2 minutes.

2. Add the Enchilada Sauce, tomatoes with chilies, tomatoes, black beans, and corn, stirring well to combine. Bring to a boil, then reduce the heat to low. Cook over low heat for 30 minutes.

3. Add the lime juice just before serving.

Substitution tip: Diced tomatoes with green chilies are usually found with the canned tomatoes in the supermarket. If you don't have any, you can substitute regular diced tomatoes and add ½ jalapeño pepper, diced, for a different kind of spicy flavor.

DAIRY-FREE • LOW-CARB • NUT-FREE
SOY-FREE • VEGAN

Per serving: Calories: 135; Fat: 3g; Carbs: 24g; Fiber: 6g; Sugar: 6g; Protein: 6g; Sodium: 96mg

Cauliflower-Potato Soup

SERVES 4

EQUIPMENT: Large pot; immersion blender or blender
PREP TIME: 15 minutes
COOK TIME: 40 minutes

This is one of my favorite comfort foods to serve on a cold or rainy day. It's a great option if you're feeding a big group because the recipe is easy to double, and it's a budget-friendly meal, too. The cauliflower helps give the soup volume but doesn't add a lot of calories and carbohydrates.

2 teaspoons olive oil

1 yellow onion, diced

4 garlic cloves, minced

4 medium russet potatoes, peeled and cut into 1-inch pieces

2 cups chopped cauliflower florets

8 cups water

4 cups whole milk

1 teaspoon salt

Freshly ground black pepper

Chopped scallions, green parts only, for garnish

1. In a large pot, heat the olive oil over medium heat for 30 seconds. Add the onion and garlic and cook for 10 minutes, stirring every minute, until the onion is translucent.

2. Add the potatoes, cauliflower, and water. Make sure the water covers the potatoes and cauliflower; add more if necessary.

3. Bring to a boil over high heat, then lower the heat and continue to simmer for 25 to 30 minutes or until the potatoes and cauliflower are fork-tender.

4. Drain the water, then add the milk and salt to the pot.

5. Blend with an immersion blender until smooth, or let cool slightly and transfer to a blender, and blend until smooth.

6. Season with additional salt and pepper to taste. Top with the scallions.

GLUTEN-FREE • NUT-FREE • SOY-FREE
DAIRY-FREE/VEGAN: *Use unsweetened soy milk instead of whole milk.*

Per serving: Calories: 341; Fat: 11g; Carbs: 51g; Fiber: 7g; Sugar: 18g; Protein: 13g; Sodium: 708mg

Curried Lentil Soup

SERVES 4
EQUIPMENT: Large pot
PREP TIME: 15 minutes
COOK TIME: 50 minutes

This curried lentil soup is full of flavor and heart-healthy protein. Lentils are one of my favorite plant-based sources of protein, so I always have a few bags of dried lentils in my pantry. They pretty much keep forever. This curried lentil soup can be made ahead of time and reheated when you're ready to enjoy it.

2 tablespoons olive oil

1 small white onion, diced

2 garlic cloves, minced

1 teaspoon curry powder

1 teaspoon turmeric

1 teaspoon ground cumin

1 (15-ounce) can low-sodium diced tomatoes

1 bay leaf

1 cup green lentils, rinsed and picked over

8 cups low-sodium vegetable broth

Salt

1. In a large pot, heat the olive oil over medium heat for 30 seconds. Add the onion and cook for 2 minutes.

2. Stir in the garlic, curry powder, turmeric, and cumin, and cook for 30 seconds. Add the tomatoes and bay leaf and cook for 2 minutes.

3. Add the lentils, stirring until well mixed, then cook for 8 minutes.

4. Raise the heat to high and add the vegetable broth. Bring to a boil, then reduce the heat to low and let simmer for 30 to 35 minutes until the lentils become soft.

5. Remove the bay leaf.

6. Season with salt to taste and serve immediately, or store in the refrigerator for up to 3 days.

Ingredient tip: Lentils aren't just a great source of protein. They're also high in soluble fiber, which can actually help lower your cholesterol. Plus they're very budget-friendly.

DAIRY-FREE • GLUTEN-FREE • LOW-CARB
NUT-FREE • SOY-FREE • VEGAN

Per serving: Calories: 211; Fat: 11g; Carbs: 16g; Fiber: 3g; Sugar: 5g; Protein: 14g; Sodium: 187mg

Rosemary White Bean Soup

SERVES 8
EQUIPMENT: Large pot
PREP TIME: 20 minutes
COOK TIME: 40 minutes

This soup takes a bit of prep work, but once you've chopped the vegetables, it comes together quite easily. This recipe makes enough to feed a crowd, but you can freeze any leftovers and reheat it for a quick and easy dinner. Serve it with some roasted sweet potatoes or a mixed green salad.

1 tablespoon olive oil

1 large white onion, diced

2 large carrots, cut into ½-inch pieces

2 celery stalks, cut into ½-inch pieces

8 garlic cloves, minced

4 cups low-sodium vegetable broth

4 cups water

2 bay leaves

1 (15-ounce) can diced tomatoes

4 (15-ounce) cans low-sodium cannellini beans, drained and rinsed

1 large rosemary sprig

Salt

Freshly ground black pepper

1. Heat the olive oil in a large pot over medium heat until the oil is shimmering. Add the onion, carrots, and celery. Reduce the heat to medium-low and cook for about 15 minutes until the vegetables begin to soften. Stir occasionally so the vegetables don't brown.

2. Add the garlic, broth, water, bay leaves, tomatoes, and beans. Simmer for 20 to 25 minutes until the vegetables are fully softened.

3. Remove from the heat and add the rosemary sprig. Stir and let sit for 15 minutes. Remove the rosemary and the bay leaves.

4. Season with salt and pepper to taste just before serving.

Substitution tip: I love cannellini beans because they're super creamy, but you can substitute great northern beans or navy beans in this recipe, if you like.

DAIRY-FREE • GLUTEN-FREE • NUT-FREE
SOY-FREE • VEGAN

Per serving: Calories: 279; Fat: 4g; Carbs: 47g; Fiber: 15g; Sugar: 8g; Protein: 17g; Sodium: 156mg

Minestrone Soup

SERVES 4

EQUIPMENT: Large pot
PREP TIME: 20 minutes
COOK TIME: 40 minutes

I love this minestrone soup because it has all the flavors of a bowl of pasta and all the nutrients of a bowl of vegetables. Sometimes I'll add in a couple handfuls of spinach at the very end of the cooking process to get a few extra greens into this soup.

1 tablespoon olive oil

1 yellow onion, diced

2 celery stalks, diced

½ cup shredded carrots

1 zucchini, chopped

1 (15-ounce) can white beans, drained and rinsed

1 (15-ounce) can diced tomatoes

2 tablespoons tomato paste

6 cups low-sodium vegetable broth

1½ teaspoons dried basil

1½ teaspoons dried oregano

Pinch salt

Pinch freshly ground black pepper

1½ cups 100 percent whole-wheat pasta shells

Handful chopped fresh basil and Italian parsley, for garnish

1. In a large pot, heat the olive oil over medium heat for 1 minute. Add the onion, celery, and carrots, and cook for 8 minutes, stirring frequently.

2. Add the zucchini, beans, tomatoes, tomato paste, vegetable broth, basil, oregano, salt, and pepper.

3. Bring to a boil, then reduce to a simmer and continue to cook for 20 minutes.

4. Add the pasta and continue to simmer for 7 to 9 minutes until the pasta is tender. Garnish with basil and parsley, if desired.

Make-ahead tip: The base of this soup can be made ahead of time. Follow the recipe except for adding the pasta. When you're ready to eat, simply reheat the soup and cook the pasta in it.

DAIRY-FREE • NUT-FREE • SOY-FREE • VEGAN

Per serving: Calories: 329; Fat: 5g; Carbs: 56g; Fiber: 12g; Sugar: 8g; Protein: 18g; Sodium: 727mg

Easy Vegan Chili

SERVES 6

EQUIPMENT: Large pot
PREP TIME: 20 minutes
COOK TIME: 35 minutes

The bulgur in this chili gives it a hearty texture without any meat. Bulgur is a whole-wheat grain that has been cracked and partially cooked. The grains are slightly smaller than rice and have a chewier texture. The splash of soy sauce adds a deep, savory flavor to the dish, so don't skip it. You can easily make this ahead of time and reheat, although you may need to add a little extra broth or water, as the chili will thicken the longer it's simmered.

1 tablespoon olive oil

1 medium yellow onion, diced

4 garlic cloves, minced

½ cup bulgur

1½ teaspoons chili powder

2 teaspoons ground cumin

½ teaspoon paprika

1 (28-ounce) can diced tomatoes

1 cup low-sodium vegetable broth

2 tablespoons tomato paste

1 teaspoon soy sauce

1 (15-ounce) can black beans, drained and rinsed

1 (15-ounce) can kidney beans, drained and rinsed

Salt

1. In a large pot, heat the olive oil over medium heat for 1 minute. Add the onion and garlic, and cook for 5 minutes until the onion is translucent.

2. Add the bulgur, chili powder, cumin, and paprika, and cook for 2 minutes.

3. Add the tomatoes, broth, tomato paste, and soy sauce, and simmer for 10 minutes.

4. Add the black beans and kidney beans, and continue to cook for 10 to 15 minutes.

5. Season with salt to taste just before serving.

Flexitarian tip: You could substitute ½ pound ground turkey for the bulgur. Just be sure to brown the turkey before adding it to the chili.

DAIRY-FREE • NUT-FREE • VEGAN

Per serving: Calories: 219; Fat: 4g; Carbs: 38g; Fiber: 12g; Sugar: 7g; Protein: 11g; Sodium: 450mg

Aloo Gobi
Indian Spiced Potatoes and Cauliflower

SERVES 2
EQUIPMENT: Large pot
PREP TIME: 15 minutes
COOK TIME: 40 minutes

Aloo gobi is one of my favorite dishes to order when we get takeout, so I decided I needed to learn how to make it at home. It's a really inexpensive dish to make and doesn't take long to assemble. You can find garam masala in the spice aisle. It's a blend of various spices that usually includes coriander, cumin, cardamom, cloves, pepper, cinnamon, and nutmeg.

1 tablespoon olive oil

1 large white onion, diced

½ teaspoon garlic powder

½ teaspoon ground ginger

2 teaspoons turmeric

1 teaspoon ground cumin

1 (15-ounce) can diced tomatoes

½ cup water, plus more if needed

1 head cauliflower, cut into 1-inch pieces

1 large russet potato, peeled and cut into 1-inch pieces

2 teaspoons garam masala

Chopped fresh cilantro, for garnish

1. In a large pot, heat the olive oil over medium heat for 30 seconds. Add the onion and cook for 8 minutes or until it is soft and translucent.

2. Add the garlic powder, ginger, turmeric, and cumin, and stir until the onion is coated.

3. Add the tomatoes, water, cauliflower, and potato, and stir. You may need to add up to ½ cup more water to ensure that the potato and cauliflower are coated.

4. Simmer for 25 to 30 minutes until the vegetables and potato are soft.

5. Add the garam masala and stir to combine.

6. Garnish with cilantro just before serving.

Substitution tip: If you want to lower the carbs in this recipe, you can replace the potato with an additional 2 cups chopped cauliflower.

DAIRY-FREE • GLUTEN-FREE • NUT-FREE
SOY-FREE • VEGAN

Per serving: Calories: 314; Fat: 8g; Carbs: 56g; Fiber: 18g; Sugar: 20g; Protein: 14g; Sodium: 152mg

Spiced Lentils and Sweet Potato Stew

SERVES 4
EQUIPMENT: Large pot
PREP TIME: 15 minutes
COOK TIME: 40 minutes

This super thick stew is quite filling and delicious. It's one of my favorite recipes to make on a cold day when I'm craving comfort food and I want something that's going to keep me energized for the rest of the day. I love serving this with the Shaved Brussels Sprouts and Pine Nuts Salad on page 58.

1 tablespoon olive oil

1 large sweet potato, peeled and cut into 1-inch pieces

2 celery stalks, diced

1 large yellow onion, diced

1 cup green lentils, rinsed and picked over

4 cups low-sodium vegetable broth, plus more if needed

1 teaspoon ground cumin

1 teaspoon garlic powder

1 teaspoon paprika

Salt

Freshly ground black pepper

1. In a large pot, heat the olive oil over medium heat. Add the sweet potato, celery, and onion, and cook for 6 minutes, stirring frequently.

2. Add the lentils, broth, cumin, garlic powder, and paprika. Bring to a boil.

3. Reduce to a simmer and simmer for 30 to 35 minutes until the lentils have softened and absorbed most of the broth. Add a bit more broth or water, if desired, for a thinner consistency. Season with salt and pepper.

DAIRY-FREE • GLUTEN-FREE • LOW-CARB
NUT-FREE • SOY-FREE • VEGAN

Per serving: Calories: 194; Fat: 5g; Carbs: 27g; Fiber: 7g; Sugar: 7g; Protein: 9g; Sodium: 79mg

Black Bean and Sweet Potato Tacos, page 93

CHAPTER 7

Wraps, Sandwiches, and Burgers

When you think of sandwiches and burgers, plant-based foods usually aren't the first things that come to mind. But there are plenty of delicious vegetarian sandwich options, and I'm excited to share a few of my favorites. Whether it's a "meaty" portobello burger or a spicy lentil wrap, these recipes will please vegetarians and meat eaters alike.

Lentil Lettuce Wraps

SERVES 4
EQUIPMENT: Large pot
PREP TIME: 20 minutes
COOK TIME: 40 minutes

The fresh ginger in this recipe provides a lot of the flavor, so don't swap it for the much milder ground stuff. For these wraps, I love using butter lettuce leaves, which are a little more tender than iceberg, but either works just fine. Add a little extra sriracha on top if you like your wraps extra spicy!

1 cup French green (*puy*) lentils, rinsed and picked over

2 garlic cloves, minced

1 yellow onion, diced

3 tablespoons soy sauce

1½ tablespoons rice wine vinegar

1 tablespoon grated fresh ginger

1 tablespoon sriracha

1 teaspoon honey

1 (8-ounce) can whole water chestnuts, drained and diced

Salt

Freshly ground black pepper

1 head iceberg or butter lettuce

2 scallions, green parts only, chopped

1. Put the lentils in a large pot and add water until it covers the lentils by ½ inch. Bring to a boil over high heat, then lower the heat and simmer for 20 to 30 minutes until the lentils are cooked. Be sure not to overcook them or they'll turn mushy.

2. Drain any excess water from the pot, then add the garlic, onion, soy sauce, vinegar, ginger, sriracha, and honey to the lentils. Cook for 3 to 4 minutes over medium heat.

3. Add the water chestnuts and continue to cook for 3 to 4 minutes. Season with salt and pepper.

4. Separate the lettuce leaves to create cups.

5. Fill each lettuce cup with ½ cup of the lentil mixture and top with a bit of the scallions. Overlap the leaves to create a wrap and close with a toothpick, if you'd like.

DAIRY-FREE • NUT-FREE
VEGAN: *Use agave nectar instead of honey.*

Per serving: Calories: 315; Fat: 0g; Carbs: 56g; Fiber: 11g; Sugar: 7g; Protein: 15g; Sodium: 816mg

Vegetable Spring Rolls

SERVES 4

EQUIPMENT: Medium pot
PREP TIME: 20 minutes
COOK TIME: 20 minutes

These spring rolls are a great way to use up vegetables you have in your refrigerator. If you're missing an ingredient, you can swap it out for cucumber or zucchini, although I recommend keeping the avocado. You can find rice paper wraps in the Asian-foods section of the grocery store.

1 cup quinoa

1 avocado

1 red bell pepper

2 tablespoons soy sauce

1 tablespoon rice vinegar

8 rice paper wraps

1 cup shredded carrots

1 cup shredded cabbage

½ cup Spicy Peanut Sauce (page 21)

Make-ahead tip: You can prepare the filling up to 2 days in advance, then assemble the spring rolls when you're ready. This is a great recipe for a party, since everyone can fill their wrap with their favorite veggies.

1. In a medium pot, cook the quinoa according to the package directions.

2. Cut the avocado and bell pepper into matchstick-size pieces.

3. When the quinoa is cooked, stir in the soy sauce and rice vinegar. Let cool.

4. Fill a large bowl or pan about halfway with warm water. Dip 1 sheet of rice paper into the warm water for about 30 seconds. The paper should still feel slightly stiff.

5. Place the wrap on a plate or glass cutting board. (It may stick to wood.) Place about 2 tablespoons of quinoa, a few pieces of avocado and bell pepper, and a pinch of carrots and cabbage on the wrap. You'll want about ⅔ cup of filling per roll. Roll up the wrap gently, tucking in the sides like a burrito.

6. Repeat with the remaining rice paper wraps, dipping them in the warm water and then filling them one at a time.

7. Serve with the Peanut Sauce.

DAIRY-FREE • VEGAN

Per serving: Calories: 303; Fat: 9g; Carbs: 48g; Fiber: 8g; Sugar: 4g; Protein: 8g; Sodium: 504mg

Spinach Falafel Wraps

SERVES 4

EQUIPMENT: Baking sheet, food processor or blender
PREP TIME: 20 minutes, plus 12 hours to soak
COOK TIME: 25 minutes

The trick here is to use dried chickpeas. Don't try to substitute canned, because you won't get the same texture and the falafel will fall apart. If you plan ahead, you'll have these wraps ready in no time.

For the falafel

1 cup dried chickpeas

6 cups water

¼ cup fresh parsley

¼ cup spinach

2 garlic cloves

1 small white onion, chopped

1 teaspoon ground coriander

1 teaspoon ground cumin

1 teaspoon salt

½ teaspoon paprika

½ teaspoon baking soda

1 tablespoon freshly squeezed lemon juice

For the wraps

4 Whole-Wheat Flatbreads (page 27) or 6-inch tortillas

1 large tomato, sliced

½ cucumber, diced

¼ cup plain Greek yogurt or tzatziki

TO MAKE THE FALAFEL

1. Cover the chickpeas with water in a large bowl. Soak for at least 12 hours, then drain.

2. Preheat the oven to 375°F. Line a baking sheet with parchment paper.

3. Combine the chickpeas, parsley, spinach, garlic, onion, coriander, cumin, salt, paprika, baking soda, and lemon juice in a food processor or blender, and blend until just slightly chunky.

4. Shape the mixture into 10 (3-inch) patties and place them on the prepared baking sheet.

5. Bake for 20 to 25 minutes until the falafel patties are brown on the bottom. They'll firm up when cooled.

TO MAKE THE WRAPS

Place 2 or 3 falafel patties into each Whole-Wheat Flatbread or wrap and top with tomato, cucumber, and tzatziki. Fold over and serve.

NUT-FREE • SOY-FREE
DAIRY-FREE/VEGAN: *Use hummus instead of tzatziki or yogurt.*
GLUTEN-FREE: *Roll up the falafel and accompaniments in steamed collard green leaves (see page 23).*

Per serving: Calories: 383; Fat: 5g; Carbs: 69g; Fiber: 15g; Sugar: 6g; Protein: 22g; Sodium: 679mg

Black Bean and Sweet Potato Tacos

SERVES 4
EQUIPMENT: Baking sheet, small saucepan
PREP TIME: 15 minutes
COOK TIME: 40 minutes

The spices give this meal tons of flavor, but you can add any toppings you like such as fresh cilantro, Greek yogurt, or shredded cheese. I love serving these tacos with the Black Bean and Avocado Salad (page 60).

1 large sweet potato or 2 small, peeled

2 teaspoons olive oil

½ teaspoon chili powder

½ teaspoon ground cumin

Pinch salt

1 (15-ounce) can black beans, with their liquid

½ teaspoon dried oregano

½ teaspoon garlic powder

8 corn tortillas

1 avocado, sliced

½ cup tomato salsa

Substitution tip: I like serving these in corn tortillas, but this filling is also great in romaine lettuce leaves or on top of Cauliflower Rice (page 25).

1. Preheat the oven to 375°F. Line a baking sheet with parchment paper.

2. Cut the sweet potato into ½-inch-thick rounds, then cut each round into quarters. In a large bowl, toss the sweet potato with the olive oil, chili powder, and cumin.

3. Spread the sweet potato in a single layer on the prepared baking sheet. Sprinkle with the salt. Roast for 20 minutes, then flip and roast for an additional 10 to 15 minutes until browned.

4. In a small saucepan, combine the black beans (with the liquid from the can) with the oregano and garlic powder, and stir.

5. Cook over low-medium heat for 10 minutes until heated through. Add salt to taste. Drain the beans.

6. Divide the sweet potatoes and black beans equally among the tortillas. Top each taco with avocado slices and tomato salsa, and any other toppings you like.

DAIRY-FREE • GLUTEN-FREE • NUT-FREE
SOY-FREE • VEGAN

Per serving: Calories: 240; Fat: 10g; Carbs: 35g; Fiber: 9g; Sugar: 8g; Protein: 6g; Sodium: 715mg

Spicy Chickpea Tacos

SERVES 4
EQUIPMENT: Baking sheet
PREP TIME: 15 minutes
COOK TIME: 35 minutes

Roasted Chickpeas (page 26) make a quick and easy taco filling. Once they're topped with creamy guacamole, you won't be able to resist. Be sure to roast the chickpeas until they're browned and crunchy. You can add an extra pinch of chili powder if you like them extra spicy.

Roasted Chickpeas (page 26)

1 tablespoon Taco Seasoning (page 16)

¼ teaspoon chili powder (optional)

2 small avocados

1 large tomato, diced

2 tablespoons diced red onion

1 jalapeño pepper, seeded and diced

Juice of ½ lime

8 6-inch tortillas

½ cup chopped fresh cilantro

1. Prepare the Roasted Chickpeas as directed, but sprinkle them with the Taco Seasoning and chili powder (if using), instead of salt before roasting.

2. While the chickpeas cook, make the guacamole: Mash the avocados in a large bowl and stir in the tomato, red onion, jalapeño pepper, and lime juice.

3. Divide the Roasted Chickpeas equally among the tortillas and top with the guacamole and cilantro.

DAIRY-FREE • GLUTEN-FREE • NUT-FREE SOY-FREE • VEGAN

Per serving: Calories: 534; Fat: 18g; Carbs: 78g; Fiber: 17g; Sugar: 3g; Protein: 16g; Sodium: 179mg

Buffalo Cauliflower Tacos

SERVES 4
EQUIPMENT: Baking sheet
PREP TIME: 10 minutes
COOK TIME: 20 minutes

Cauliflower is an amazing base for this kind of sauce, and once you put it in a taco . . . well, it doesn't get much better than that. The ranch dressing is totally optional, but I love the way it balances out the fiery cauliflower. If ranch dressing is not your thing, try Greek yogurt or salsa.

For the ranch dressing

2 tablespoons mayonnaise

1 tablespoon milk

¼ teaspoon dried dill

¼ teaspoon garlic powder

Salt

Freshly ground black pepper

For the tacos

1 cup Buffalo-style hot sauce

2 tablespoons olive oil

2 teaspoons paprika

1 head cauliflower, cut into 1-inch florets

8 large romaine lettuce leaves

½ cup shredded purple cabbage

Substitution tip: You can assemble these tacos in corn tortillas if you prefer, but lettuce leaves are a great low-carb alternative.

TO MAKE THE DRESSING

Whisk the mayonnaise and milk together in a medium bowl. Stir in the dill and garlic powder. Season with salt and pepper.

TO MAKE THE TACOS

1. Preheat the oven to 425°F. Line a baking sheet with parchment paper.

2. In a large bowl, combine the hot sauce, olive oil, and paprika. Add the cauliflower and toss to coat.

3. Spread the cauliflower on the prepared baking sheet and roast for 10 minutes, then flip and continue roasting for another 5 to 10 minutes, until the cauliflower has started to brown.

4. Wash and dry the lettuce leaves, and trim off the white ends. Divide the cauliflower and cabbage equally among the lettuce leaves, similar to filling a taco shell, and top with the ranch dressing. Serve immediately.

GLUTEN-FREE • LOW-CARB • NUT-FREE • SOY-FREE
DAIRY-FREE/VEGAN: *Use vegan mayonnaise and either soy or almond milk in the ranch dressing.*

Per serving: Calories: 118; Fat: 10g; Carbs: 8g; Fiber: 2g; Sugar: 3g; Protein: 2g; Sodium: 1677mg

Smashed White Bean and Avocado Sandwiches

SERVES 2
PREP TIME: 10 minutes

This is such a fast and easy recipe, it's great for a quick lunch! I think this sandwich is delicious served on toasted whole-grain bread, but you can also use this filling instead of the tabbouleh in Collard Green Wraps (page 23). It tastes great spread onto a whole-grain pita, too.

1 (15-ounce) can white beans, drained and rinsed

1 avocado

Juice of 1 lemon

½ teaspoon salt

½ teaspoon garlic powder

¼ teaspoon onion powder

Pinch freshly ground black pepper

4 slices whole-grain bread

½ cup shredded carrots

8 slices cucumber

1. In a large bowl, mash the white beans and avocado with a fork until mixed but still chunky.

2. Stir in the lemon juice, then add the salt, garlic powder, onion powder, and pepper. Stir to combine.

3. Toast the slices of bread until slightly brown.

4. Spread half of the bean mixture on 1 slice of toasted bread, add half of the carrots and cucumber slices, and top with another slice of toast. Repeat.

DAIRY-FREE • NUT-FREE • SOY-FREE • VEGAN

Per serving: Calories: 488; Fat: 22g; Carbs: 58g; Fiber: 22g; Sugar: 7g; Protein: 18g; Sodium: 976mg

Spicy Black Bean Burgers

SERVES 4

EQUIPMENT: Baking sheet, blender or food processor
PREP TIME: 15 minutes
COOK TIME: 30 minutes

I love how flavorful these burgers are, and I typically eat them without a bun, topped with salsa and avocado. If you want more of a traditional burger, serve them with whole-wheat hamburger buns and your favorite toppings. Be sure to drain the beans as much as possible, or the mixture will be too wet.

1 medium yellow onion, chopped

1 (15-ounce) can sweet corn, drained

1 (15-ounce) can black beans, rinsed and drained

⅓ cup rolled oats

1 teaspoon dried oregano

4 teaspoons chili powder

1 teaspoon ground cumin

¼ cup chopped fresh parsley

1 teaspoon salt

1. Preheat the oven to 350°F. Line a baking sheet with parchment paper.

2. Put the onion, corn, beans, oats, oregano, chili powder, cumin, parsley, and salt in a blender or food processor and pulse 10 to 15 times until the ingredients are combined but still chunky.

3. Shape the mixture into 4 large patties and place them on the prepared baking sheet. They will be wet, but the patties should hold their shape.

4. Bake for 25 to 30 minutes until browned on the bottom and firmly set.

Make-ahead tip: These burgers can be made in advance and frozen. Simply let them cool, then freeze in a single layer. Be sure not to stack them before freezing, or they'll stick together.

DAIRY-FREE • GLUTEN-FREE • NUT-FREE
SOY-FREE • VEGAN

Per serving: Calories: 171; Fat: 2g; Carbs: 34g; Fiber: 7g; Sugar: 4g; Protein: 7g; Sodium: 864mg

Portobello Burgers

SERVES 4

EQUIPMENT: Large skillet or grill pan

PREP TIME: 15 minutes, plus 1 hour to marinate

COOK TIME: 10 minutes

Portobello mushrooms have a great texture as burger replacements, but it takes a little work to infuse them with flavor. Marinate the mushrooms in the seasoning for at least an hour before preparing, or overnight in the refrigerator, then brush on the remaining marinade while cooking. Use a heavy skillet to cook them; a cast-iron skillet is ideal. You can serve these just like traditional burgers.

4 large portobello mushrooms

¼ cup olive oil

2 tablespoons soy sauce

¼ teaspoon garlic powder

Salt

Freshly ground black pepper

4 100 percent whole-wheat buns

4 large lettuce leaves

4 large slices red onion

4 slices tomato

1 avocado, sliced

1. Gently twist the stem of each mushroom to remove it. Use a small spoon to scrape the gills off the underside of the mushrooms. Wipe the caps with a damp paper towel to remove any dirt.

2. Using a sharp knife, lightly score the top of each mushroom with a crosshatch pattern. You want to just barely cut through the surface. This will help the mushroom absorb more marinade.

3. In a large zip-top bag, combine the olive oil, soy sauce, and garlic powder. Seal the bag and shake. Then add the mushrooms to the bag and gently shift them until they're coated with the mixture. Set aside to marinate for at least 1 hour.

4. Heat a large skillet or grill pan over medium heat for 1 minute.

5. Remove the mushrooms from the zip-top bag, but reserve the marinade. Place each mushroom in the skillet, brush with marinade, and cook for 5 minutes. Flip and continue to cook for 5 to 7 minutes, brushing with more marinade.

6. Season with salt and pepper, and place each mushroom on a bun.

7. Top each burger with 1 lettuce leaf, 1 red onion slice, 1 tomato slice, and 1 or 2 avocado slices.

DAIRY-FREE • NUT-FREE • VEGAN

Per serving: Calories: 370; Fat: 24g; Carbs: 33g; Fiber: 9g; Sugar: 4g; Protein: 12g; Sodium: 734mg

Acorn Squash Stuffed with Barley, page 110

CHAPTER 8

Roasted and Baked Dinners

It's amazing how roasting or baking a vegetable can completely transform it. These recipes bring out the delicious depth of flavor in some of my favorite vegetables. Many of these recipes require just one pot or pan, to make cleaning up quick and easy. From enchiladas to acorn squash, these plant-based dishes are some of my favorite dinners.

Roasted Vegetables and Chickpeas

SERVES 4
EQUIPMENT: Two baking sheets
PREP TIME: 15 minutes
COOK TIME: 35 minutes

In my house, we have a variation of this nearly once a week, especially in the winter. I love the combination of sweet potatoes and asparagus, but you can also make this with red potatoes and broccoli. For a variation on the spices, try substituting fresh dill for the cumin.

2 (15-ounce) cans chickpeas, rinsed and drained

1 large sweet potato, peeled and cut into ½-inch chunks

2 tablespoons olive oil, divided

3 garlic cloves, minced

1 teaspoon ground cumin

1 pound asparagus, ends trimmed

Salt

Freshly ground black pepper

Juice of ½ lemon

1. Preheat the oven to 450°F. Line two baking sheets with parchment paper.

2. In a large bowl, toss the chickpeas and sweet potato with 1½ tablespoons of olive oil and the garlic and cumin.

3. Spread the chickpeas and sweet potato on one of the prepared baking sheets and roast for 20 minutes.

4. Meanwhile, lay the asparagus on the other prepared baking sheet and drizzle with the remaining ½ tablespoon of olive oil.

5. After the chickpeas and sweet potato have been roasting for 20 minutes, flip the sweet potato and stir the chickpeas, and continue to roast along with the asparagus for 10 to 15 minutes until the chickpeas and sweet potato are crispy and the asparagus is lightly browned.

6. Season with salt and pepper. Sprinkle the lemon juice over the asparagus and chickpeas.

DAIRY-FREE • GLUTEN-FREE • NUT-FREE
SOY-FREE • VEGAN

Per serving: Calories: 416; Fat: 10g; Carbs: 69g; Fiber: 15g; Sugar: 5g; Protein: 16g; Sodium: 777mg

Bell Pepper Nachos

SERVES 4 TO 6
EQUIPMENT: Baking sheet
PREP TIME: 10 minutes
COOK TIME: 20 minutes

These bell pepper nachos are a healthier alternative to your favorite game-day nachos. Swapping slices of bell pepper for chips is an easy way to make this a lower-carb dish. A handful of cheese makes these nachos feel indulgent, but this recipe is packed with healthy ingredients. Serve alongside Cauliflower Rice (page 25) to make a complete meal.

4 bell peppers

½ teaspoon ground cumin

½ teaspoon chili powder

¼ teaspoon garlic powder

1 cup canned black beans, rinsed and drained

½ cup shredded Cheddar cheese

2 avocados, diced

½ cup pico de gallo

¼ cup diced jalapeño pepper (optional)

Ingredient tip: Pico de gallo is a salsa that is typically made with chopped fresh tomatoes, onion, and cilantro. It's usually sold in the refrigerated section of the grocery store near the precut vegetables. Look for a brand with all-natural ingredients. You can substitute jarred salsa, if you prefer.

1. Preheat the oven to 425°F. Line a baking sheet with parchment paper.

2. Cut the peppers into quarters and remove the seeds and pith. Cut each quarter into 2-inch-wide wedges. In a large bowl, toss the peppers with the cumin, chili powder, and garlic powder.

3. Spread the bell peppers on the prepared baking sheet and roast for 5 to 7 minutes until they're tender but still crisp.

4. Using a spatula, heap the bell peppers in a pile in the center of the baking sheet, then top them with the beans and cheese.

5. Continue to roast for another 8 to 10 minutes until the cheese has melted.

6. Top with the avocado, pico de gallo, and jalapeño pepper (if using).

GLUTEN-FREE • LOW-CARB • NUT-FREE • SOY-FREE
DAIRY-FREE/VEGAN: *Substitute vegan shredded Cheddar cheese.*

Per serving: Calories: 314; Fat: 25g; Carbs: 19g; Fiber: 10g; Sugar: 4g; Protein: 8g; Sodium: 201mg

Easy Ratatouille

SERVES 4
EQUIPMENT: Large skillet
PREP TIME: 15 minutes
COOK TIME: 35 minutes

This dish requires very little preparation other than chopping the vegetables, but the end result is colorful and delicious. While this dish cooks on the stove top rather than the oven, I think you'll find the end result to be just as filling and comforting as the other recipes in this chapter. I love eating this ratatouille with some crusty bread and a sprinkle of Parmesan cheese. It's also delicious served over pasta!

1 tablespoon olive oil

1 large white onion, diced

3 garlic cloves, minced

1 (28-ounce) can whole tomatoes

1 bunch fresh thyme, tied with kitchen string

1 medium eggplant, cut into 1-inch cubes

1 medium zucchini, halved lengthwise, then cut into 1-inch pieces

1 medium yellow squash, halved lengthwise, then cut into 1-inch pieces

1 teaspoon salt

Handful fresh basil, cut into ribbons

1. In a large skillet, heat the olive oil over medium heat for 1 minute until it begins to shimmer. Add the onion and cook for 5 minutes. Add the garlic and continue cooking for another 3 minutes.

2. Add the tomatoes and bundle of thyme. Let them cook for about 5 minutes over low to medium heat, using a spoon to gently break apart the tomatoes.

3. Add the eggplant, zucchini, and yellow squash, and continue cooking for 20 minutes or until the vegetables have softened.

4. Remove the thyme. Season with salt and top with the basil just before serving.

DAIRY-FREE • GLUTEN-FREE • LOW-CARB
NUT-FREE • SOY-FREE • VEGAN

Per serving: Calories: 128; Fat: 4g; Carbs: 22g; Fiber: 8g; Sugar: 12g; Protein: 5g; Sodium: 605mg

Mexican Quinoa Bake

SERVES 6

EQUIPMENT: 8-by-8-inch baking dish, medium pot, large pan
PREP TIME: 15 minutes
COOK TIME: 35 minutes

If you hate meal prepping, you'll love this recipe. It takes only a few minutes of prep before you have this in the oven, and it reheats well. You can customize this dish with any toppings you like, including plain Greek yogurt. My favorites are avocado, fresh cilantro, and a little extra salsa.

Nonstick cooking spray

1 cup quinoa, rinsed

2 cups low-sodium vegetable broth

1 teaspoon olive oil

1 bell pepper, seeded and diced

1 small yellow onion, diced

1 cup tomato salsa

1 (15-ounce) can salt-free black beans, drained and rinsed

1 cup salt-free corn kernels, fresh, canned, or frozen (thawed)

1 teaspoon ground cumin

½ teaspoon chili powder (optional)

Salt

1. Preheat the oven to 400°F. Spray an 8-by-8-inch baking dish with nonstick cooking spray.

2. In a medium pot, bring the quinoa and vegetable broth to a boil. Let it simmer for 10 to 12 minutes until the broth is completely absorbed.

3. Meanwhile, in a large pan, heat the olive oil over medium heat. Add the bell pepper and onion. Cook for 5 to 7 minutes until it just begins to soften. Remove from the heat and set aside.

4. When the quinoa is cooked, stir in the salsa, black beans, corn, cumin, cooked bell pepper and onion, and chili powder (if using). Season with salt.

5. Pour the quinoa mixture into the prepared baking dish. Bake for 15 minutes until heated through.

6. Top with whatever toppings you like.

DAIRY-FREE • GLUTEN-FREE • NUT-FREE
SOY-FREE • VEGAN

Per serving: Calories: 336; Fat: 6g; Carbs: 57g; Fiber: 8g; Sugar: 2g; Protein: 14g; Sodium: 218mg

Flexitarian tip: If you want to add meat to this dish, brown 1 pound of ground turkey in the pan before cooking the pepper and onion. Then combine the turkey with the cooked vegetables and continue the recipe. This would increase the yield to 8 servings.

Black Bean Enchiladas

EQUIPMENT: 8-by-8-inch baking dish
PREP TIME: 15 minutes
COOK TIME: 20 minutes

Rather than using cheese as the enchilada filling, I use refried beans, which creates a creamy texture with less saturated fat and more fiber. Be sure to look for vegetarian refried beans, because traditional refried beans contain animal fat. You can top this dish with fresh cilantro, salsa, avocado, Greek yogurt, a little shredded cheese, or anything else you like.

Nonstick cooking spray

1 (15-ounce) can black beans, drained and rinsed

½ teaspoon ground cumin

½ teaspoon garlic powder

¼ teaspoon dried oregano

1 (15-ounce) can vegetarian refried beans

2 teaspoons Taco Seasoning (page 16)

8 corn tortillas

1 cup Enchilada Sauce (page 22)

Prep tip: Wrap the corn tortillas in a damp paper towel and microwave for 30 seconds. This will lightly steam them so you can roll them without any cracking.

1. Preheat the oven to 400°F. Spray an 8-by-8-inch baking dish with nonstick cooking spray.

2. In a large bowl, combine the black beans with the cumin, garlic powder, and oregano.

3. In a medium bowl, mix the refried beans with the Taco Seasoning.

4. Fill each tortilla with a few tablespoons of black beans and 2 tablespoons of refried beans. Don't fill them too full or they'll split when you roll them up.

5. Roll each enchilada and place it in the baking dish, seam-side down. Line them up to the edges of the baking dish. Pour the Enchilada Sauce over the tortillas.

6. Cover with aluminum foil and bake for 15 minutes. Remove the foil and bake for 5–10 minutes more until the sauce is bubbly.

7. Let stand for a few minutes before serving with the toppings of your choice.

DAIRY-FREE • NUT-FREE • SOY-FREE • VEGAN

Per serving: Calories: 333; Fat: 8g; Carbs: 57g; Fiber: 13g; Sugar: 2g; Protein: 14g; Sodium: 867mg

The Truly Healthy Vegetarian Cookbook

Oven-Roasted Portobello Fajitas

SERVES 4

EQUIPMENT: 2 or 3 nonstick baking sheets, small saucepan
PREP TIME: 15 minutes
COOK TIME: 35 minutes

You'll need more than one pan to spread out the vegetables for roasting, but be aware that the portobello mushrooms will shrink as they cook. Be sure to use vegetarian refried beans, as traditional beans are made with lard. Top these fajitas with salsa, fresh cilantro, diced avocado, Greek yogurt, or anything else you'd like.

4 bell peppers, any color, seeded and cut into ¼-inch strips

3 teaspoons olive oil, divided

2 teaspoons Taco Seasoning (page 16), divided

6 portobello mushrooms, stems removed, caps sliced into ¼-inch strips

1 (15-ounce) can vegetarian refried beans

8 corn tortillas

1. Preheat the oven to 400°F. Line 2 baking sheets with parchment paper.

2. In a medium bowl, drizzle the bell peppers with 1½ teaspoons of olive oil, then toss with 1 teaspoon of Taco Seasoning. Spread the bell peppers on one of the prepared baking sheets and roast for 15 minutes.

3. Meanwhile, in a large bowl, drizzle the mushrooms with the remaining 1½ teaspoons of olive oil and toss with the remaining 1 teaspoon of Taco Seasoning. Spread the mushrooms on the second prepared baking sheet. If needed, line a third baking sheet with parchment paper and spread the rest of the mushrooms on it.

4. After the bell peppers have been cooking for 15 minutes, roast the portobello mushrooms along with the bell peppers for 10 minutes. Stir the bell peppers and mushrooms and continue to roast for 10 minutes more or until browned.

CONTINUED

5. During the final 10 minutes of roasting, heat the refried beans in a small saucepan over medium heat, stirring until heated through, 7 to 8 minutes.

6. Top the corn tortillas with the refried beans, then the mushrooms and peppers and any additional toppings of your choice.

Substitution tip: To make this a lower-carb meal, skip the tortillas and serve in a bowl with some diced avocado and salsa.

DAIRY-FREE • GLUTEN-FREE • NUT-FREE
SOY-FREE • VEGAN

Per serving: Calories: 295; Fat: 6g; Carbs: 51g; Fiber: 10g; Sugar: 1g; Protein: 13g; Sodium: 460mg

Peppers Stuffed with Mexican Cauliflower Rice

SERVES 4

EQUIPMENT: Medium saucepan, large casserole dish
PREP TIME: 30 minutes
COOK TIME: 45 minutes

Cauliflower rice makes a delicious filling for stuffed peppers. You might not even notice it's not regular rice! The filling is also great inside tacos.

Nonstick cooking spray

1 tablespoon olive oil

2 garlic cloves, minced

¼ cup diced bell pepper, any color

¼ cup diced yellow onion

2 tablespoons tomato paste

3 cups cooked Cauliflower Rice (page 25)

1 (15-ounce) can black beans, drained and rinsed

½ cup tomato salsa

4 whole bell peppers, halved lengthwise and seeded

½ cup shredded Cheddar cheese (optional)

Flexitarian tip: Trade the black beans for the same amount of cooked ground turkey.

1. Preheat the oven to 375°F. Spray a large casserole dish with nonstick cooking spray.

2. In a medium saucepan, heat the olive oil over medium heat until shimmering, about 1 minute. Add the garlic, diced bell pepper, and onion, and cook for 1 minute. Add the tomato paste and stir well.

3. Stir in the cauliflower. Continue to cook for 2 minutes until the cauliflower just begins to soften. Do not overcook or the cauliflower will become too soft.

4. In a large bowl, combine the cooked Cauliflower Rice with the black beans and salsa.

5. Stuff the bell peppers with the cauliflower mixture and place them stuffed-side up in the prepared casserole dish. Top with the cheese (if using). Cover with aluminum foil and bake for 30 minutes.

6. Remove the foil and increase the temperature to 400°F. Continue to cook for 10 minutes more.

GLUTEN-FREE • LOW-CARB • NUT-FREE • SOY-FREE
DAIRY-FREE/VEGAN: *Leave out the cheese.*

Per serving: Calories: 153; Fat: 4g; Carbs: 24g; Fiber: 6g; Sugar: 9g; Protein: 6g; Sodium: 498mg

Acorn Squash Stuffed with Barley

SERVES 4
EQUIPMENT: Baking sheet, large pot
PREP TIME: 30 minutes
COOK TIME: 50 minutes

Not only is this acorn squash dish delicious, but the presentation is lovely as well. The barley takes time to cook, but it's worth the wait!

2 acorn squash, halved lengthwise and seeded

3 teaspoons olive oil, divided

1 yellow onion, diced

4 garlic cloves, minced

4 cups vegetable broth, divided

1 tablespoon freshly squeezed lemon juice

1½ cups barley

1 teaspoon fresh thyme leaves or ¼ teaspoon dried thyme, plus more for garnish

3 cups water

2 tablespoons toasted pine nuts

Handful microgreens and pomegranate seeds, for garnish (optional)

Prep tip: To toast pine nuts, put them in a dry skillet and cook over medium heat for 2 to 3 minutes, stirring frequently, until lightly browned.

1. Preheat the oven to 400°F. Line a baking sheet with parchment paper.

2. Brush the inside of the squash with 1 teaspoon of olive oil. Arrange the halves cut-side down on the prepared baking sheet and roast for 45 to 50 minutes until soft on the inside.

3. Meanwhile, in a large pot, heat the remaining 2 teaspoons of olive oil over medium heat. Add the onion and garlic and cook for 5 minutes until the onion begins to soften. Add ½ cup of vegetable broth and the lemon juice, barley, and thyme.

4. Let the barley absorb the stock, 3 to 4 minutes. When it does, add another ½ cup of stock. Continue to add the stock ½ cup at a time, waiting until the barley has absorbed most of it before adding more. Once all the stock has been absorbed, add the water, ½ cup at a time, until the barley is tender. Overall, the barley will take about 45 minutes to cook.

5. When the squash has finished roasting, spoon a quarter of the barley mixture into each squash half.

6. Garnish with thyme, pine nuts, and microgreens and pomegranate seeds (if using).

DAIRY-FREE • SOY-FREE • VEGAN

Per serving: Calories: 445; Fat: 10g; Carbs: 78g; Fiber: 16g; Sugar: 3g; Protein: 16g; Sodium: 781mg

Eggplant Ricotta Roll-Ups

SERVES 4

EQUIPMENT: 2 baking sheets, 8-by-8-inch baking dish

PREP TIME: 30 minutes

COOK TIME: 50 minutes

If you love lasagna but you're looking for a lower-carb option, try these eggplant roll-ups. I like to broil this dish for just a couple of minutes at the end of the baking time, until the cheese is bubbly and browned. When buying marinara sauce, check the ingredients to be sure it doesn't have added sugar. Look for a sauce that contains nothing but tomatoes, olive oil, herbs, and spices.

2 medium eggplants

Salt

1 cup ricotta cheese

¼ teaspoon dried oregano

¼ teaspoon dried parsley

2 cups marinara sauce, divided

2 cups fresh baby spinach

½ cup shredded mozzarella cheese

¼ cup fresh basil leaves, cut into ribbons

1. Preheat the oven to 350°F. Line 2 baking sheets with parchment paper.

2. Cut the stem ends off the eggplants, then carefully cut the eggplants lengthwise into ¼-inch slices. Spread the eggplant slices on the prepared baking sheets, season with salt, and let sit for 20 minutes to release their moisture. Pat the slices dry with a paper towel.

3. Bake the eggplant slices for 20 minutes or until they've softened. Let cool.

4. While the eggplant cooks, combine the ricotta, oregano, and parsley in a large bowl.

5. Increase the oven temperature to 400°F.

6. Pour ½ cup of marinara sauce into an 8-by-8-inch baking dish and spread it evenly over the bottom.

CONTINUED

7. Spoon 2 tablespoons of ricotta mixture onto 1 eggplant slice near the narrow end of the eggplant, then add a small handful of spinach. Roll up the eggplant slice and place it in the baking dish, seam-side down. Repeat with the remaining slices, then cover the roll-ups with the remaining 1½ cups of marinara sauce. Sprinkle with the mozzarella cheese.

8. Bake for 20 to 25 minutes until the cheese has completely melted. If desired, set the oven to broil for 2 to 3 minutes until the cheese is bubbly and browned.

9. Top with the basil just before serving.

Prep tip: Salting and baking the eggplant first helps remove moisture, so your final dish isn't watery or bitter.

GLUTEN-FREE • LOW-CARB • NUT-FREE • SOY-FREE
DAIRY-FREE/VEGAN: *Use tofu ricotta instead of the cheese and leave out the mozzarella. Drizzle with olive oil just before serving.*

Per serving: Calories: 203; Fat: 7g; Carbs: 25g; Fiber: 11g; Sugar: 12g; Protein: 12g; Sodium: 396mg

Gigantes Plaki
Giant Baked Beans

SERVES 4

EQUIPMENT: Large pot, 8-by-8-inch baking dish

PREP TIME: 10 minutes

COOK TIME: 50 minutes

Gigantes plaki is a traditional Greek dish that uses large butter beans. If you can't find butter beans, you can use large lima beans instead. This is a super simple dish that can be served on its own or with feta cheese and freshly baked bread.

4 tablespoons olive oil, divided

1 large yellow onion, diced

4 garlic cloves, thinly sliced

2 (15-ounce) cans diced tomatoes

2 (15-ounce) cans large butter beans, drained and rinsed

1 teaspoon dried thyme

1. Preheat the oven to 425°F.

2. In a large pot, heat 2 tablespoons of olive oil over low heat for 1 minute. Add the onion and garlic and cook for 4 to 5 minutes, stirring occasionally, until the onion is translucent.

3. Add the tomatoes and simmer for 10 minutes. Add the butter beans and thyme, and stir to coat the beans with the sauce.

4. Pour the tomato and bean mixture into an 8-by-8-inch baking dish and drizzle with the remaining 2 tablespoons of olive oil.

5. Bake, uncovered, for 30 to 35 minutes until the beans are completely heated through.

DAIRY-FREE • GLUTEN-FREE • NUT-FREE
SOY-FREE • VEGAN

Per serving: Calories: 357; Fat: 14g; Carbs: 49g; Fiber: 15g; Sugar: 7g; Protein: 14g; Sodium: 822mg

Pesto Zucchini Noodles, page 117

CHAPTER 9

Noodles, Rice, and Pasta

When you think of pasta or rice, you might think of carb-heavy meals with little nutritional value. But this chapter is packed with vegetable-forward meals. In many recipes, I've indicated where you could use spaghetti squash or Zucchini Noodles (page 24) instead of traditional pasta. I also love using chickpea noodles, which are simply noodles made from chickpea flour. They're gaining in popularity as a pasta alternative, with additional protein and fiber.

Cauliflower Rice Burrito Bowls

SERVES 4
EQUIPMENT: Small pot
PREP TIME: 30 minutes
COOK TIME: 20 minutes

These cauliflower burrito bowls can really be customized however you like. Feel free to add hot sauce, plain Greek yogurt, salsa verde, or any other burrito toppings you love. Sometimes I'll combine this recipe with Oven-Roasted Portobello Fajitas (page 107) and serve the fajitas over Cauliflower Rice (page 25). You really can't go wrong with this burrito bowl recipe as a starting point.

4 cups Cauliflower Rice (page 25)

¼ cup lime juice

½ cup chopped fresh cilantro

½ teaspoon salt

2 (15-ounce) cans black beans, drained and rinsed

2 teaspoons dried oregano

2 teaspoons ground cumin

2 avocados

¼ cup diced red onion

½ jalapeño pepper, seeded and diced

Salt

1 cup pico de gallo

1. Prepare the Cauliflower Rice as directed.

2. In a large bowl, toss the Cauliflower Rice with the lime juice, cilantro, and salt.

3. In a small pot, combine the black beans, oregano, and cumin and cook over medium-low heat for 5 to 7 minutes until the beans are heated through.

4. In another large bowl, mash the avocados with a fork. Add the red onion and jalapeño pepper, and stir gently to combine. Season with salt.

5. Divide the Cauliflower Rice among four bowls. Top each with a quarter of the black beans, avocado mixture, and pico de gallo.

Ingredient tip: Cauliflower Rice has more moisture than regular rice, so it's best served with chunky salsas and toppings rather than watery sauces. I like using pico de gallo because it doesn't add a lot of moisture.

DAIRY-FREE • GLUTEN-FREE • NUT-FREE
SOY-FREE • VEGAN

Per serving: Calories: 378; Fat: 21g; Carbs: 40g; Fiber: 17g; Sugar: 6g; Protein: 16g; Sodium: 770mg

Pesto Zucchini Noodles

SERVES 4

EQUIPMENT: Blender or food processor
PREP TIME: 5 minutes

Zucchini Noodles (page 24) can get soggy if they're served with a watery sauce, which is why I love topping them with pesto. This dish is delicious served warm or cold. You can even leave the zucchini raw, if you like more of a crunch.

Zucchini Noodles (page 24)

¼ cup walnuts

½ cup olive oil

½ cup loosely packed
fresh basil

1 garlic clove

¾ teaspoon balsamic vinegar

¼ cup grated
Parmesan cheese

Salt

1. Prepare the Zucchini Noodles as directed.

2. In a blender or food processor, process the walnuts, olive oil, basil, garlic, vinegar, and Parmesan cheese to a smooth pesto consistency.

3. Divide the Zucchini Noodles into 4 servings. Toss each serving with 2 tablespoons of pesto. Season with salt.

GLUTEN-FREE • LOW-CARB • SOY-FREE
DAIRY-FREE/VEGAN: *Use 2 tablespoons nutritional yeast instead of the Parmesan cheese. Add more salt, if necessary.*

Per serving: Calories: 341; Fat: 32g; Carbs: 12g; Fiber: 4g; Sugar: 6g; Protein: 7g; Sodium: 137mg

Red Lentil Bolognese

SERVES 4

EQUIPMENT: Baking sheet, blender or food processor, large skillet
PREP TIME: 15 minutes
COOK TIME: 45 minutes

The hearty sauce in this dish can also be served over Zucchini Noodles (page 24) or traditional pasta.

2 medium spaghetti squash (3 to 4 pounds each), halved lengthwise and seeded

2 celery stalks, cut into 2-inch pieces

1 medium white onion, cut into 2-inch pieces

2 carrots, cut into 2-inch pieces

4 garlic cloves

1 tablespoon olive oil

⅔ cup red lentils, rinsed and picked over

1 (28-ounce) can diced tomatoes

¼ cup low-sodium vegetable broth, plus more if needed

1 cup marinara sauce or tomato sauce

½ teaspoon dried basil

½ teaspoon dried parsley

½ teaspoon dried oregano

¼ teaspoon red pepper flakes (optional)

1. Preheat the oven to 400°F. Line a baking sheet with parchment paper.

2. Place the squash halves cut-side down on the prepared baking sheet. Bake for 40 to 45 minutes until you can separate the strands with a fork.

3. Meanwhile, pulse the celery, onion, carrots, and garlic in a blender or food processor until just slightly chunky.

4. In a large skillet, heat the olive oil over medium heat. Add the vegetable mixture and cook for 6 minutes. Add the lentils, tomatoes, and broth, and cook for 15 minutes. Add the marinara sauce, basil, parsley, oregano, and red pepper flakes (if using). Cook for 5 to 10 minutes until the lentils are soft. If they begin to stick, add a splash more vegetable stock.

5. When the squash is roasted, carefully scrape the insides with a fork to form noodles.

6. Divide the noodles among four bowls and top with the sauce.

DAIRY-FREE • GLUTEN-FREE • NUT-FREE SOY-FREE • VEGAN

Per serving: Calories: 346; Fat: 7g; Carbs: 60g; Fiber: 16g; Sugar: 14g; Protein: 14g; Sodium: 397mg

Ingredient tip: Lentils are full of fiber and complex carbohydrates, so they provide slow-burning energy for hours.

Stuffed Spaghetti Squash

SERVES 4
EQUIPMENT: Baking sheet
PREP TIME: 10 minutes
COOK TIME: 35 minutes

This spaghetti squash has all the flavor of lasagna without all the carbs and calories! You can also serve this dish right in the squash halves, which makes cleanup a breeze.

2 small spaghetti squash (2 to 3 pounds each), halved lengthwise and seeded

1 teaspoon olive oil

2 garlic cloves, halved lengthwise

1 cup marinara sauce

1 cup ricotta cheese

1 cup chopped fresh spinach

¾ cup shredded mozzarella cheese

Handful chopped fresh basil

Prep tip: Raw spaghetti squash can be difficult to cut, even with a sharp knife. To soften the skin and make it easier to cut, pierce the squash all around with a fork, then microwave for 3 to 4 minutes.

1. Preheat the oven to 400°F. Line a baking sheet with parchment paper.

2. Brush the insides of the squash with the olive oil and rub with the garlic. Place the halves cut-side down on the prepared baking sheet and bake for 20 to 30 minutes until the flesh is slightly soft and translucent.

3. Meanwhile, in a large bowl, mix the marinara sauce, ricotta, and spinach.

4. Once the squash is roasted, carefully scrape the insides with a fork to form spaghetti-like noodles.

5. Spoon a quarter of the marinara mixture into each squash half and mix with the squash strands. Top each squash half with 3 tablespoons of mozzarella.

6. Broil the squash for 3 to 4 minutes until the cheese is bubbly and slightly browned.

7. Let cool for 2 to 3 minutes. Top with the basil and serve.

GLUTEN-FREE • LOW-CARB • NUT-FREE • SOY-FREE DAIRY-FREE/VEGAN: *Use vegan ricotta and skip the mozzarella. Drizzle with olive oil before serving.*

Per serving: Calories: 247; Fat: 10g; Carbs: 30g; Fiber: 2g; Sugar: 6g; Protein: 12g; Sodium: 415mg

Spicy Soba Noodles

SERVES 4
EQUIPMENT: Large pot
PREP TIME: 10 minutes
COOK TIME: 10 minutes

Soba noodles are often served cold, although I prefer these warm. If you'd rather serve them cold, you can skip the last step, where you cook the noodles and sauce together. Instead, simply rinse the noodles in cold water after cooking, then serve the sauce on the side.

8 ounces soba noodles

1½ tablespoons soy sauce

1½ tablespoons sesame oil

2 teaspoons rice vinegar

1½ tablespoons honey

¼ teaspoon sriracha, plus more to taste

2 cups shelled edamame

1. Bring a large pot of water to a boil. Cook the soba noodles according to the package directions.

2. While the noodles cook, whisk together the soy sauce, sesame oil, vinegar, honey, and sriracha in a small bowl.

3. Drain the noodles, then return them to the pot.

4. Stir in the sauce and edamame, and continue to cook over medium heat for 2 minutes, stirring until the sauce has thickened and the edamame is warm.

Substitution tip: If you can't find soba noodles, you can substitute whole-wheat spaghetti noodles, which have a similar texture.

DAIRY-FREE • NUT-FREE

VEGAN: *Substitute agave nectar for the honey.*

Per serving: Calories: 354; Fat: 9g; Carbs: 56g; Fiber: 2g; Sugar: 8g; Protein: 16g; Sodium: 801mg

Broccoli Fried Rice with Tempeh

SERVES 4

EQUIPMENT: Large nonstick skillet

PREP TIME: 15 minutes, plus 2 hours to marinate

COOK TIME: 20 minutes

Tempeh is a great source of protein, and it's easy to prepare. With a little marinating, it takes on tons of flavor, which is perfect with this fried rice. If you've been hesitant to try it, give this recipe a shot. Tempeh is typically found in the refrigerated section of the grocery store near the tofu.

---

2 (8-ounce) packages tempeh

½ cup low-sodium soy sauce, divided

2 tablespoons maple syrup

2 tablespoons avocado oil, divided

3 cups cooked brown rice, cold or room temperature

1 egg

1 cup broccoli florets, fresh or frozen

½ cup corn kernels, fresh or frozen

½ cup peas, fresh or frozen

1 garlic clove, minced

1 teaspoon grated fresh ginger

1. Cut the tempeh into ¼-inch strips. Place them in a shallow dish large enough to hold them in a single layer.

2. In a small bowl, whisk together ¼ cup of soy sauce and the maple syrup. Drizzle the sauce over the tempeh, turning each piece to ensure it is evenly coated. Cover with plastic wrap and marinate for at least 2 hours, or overnight, in the refrigerator.

3. In a large nonstick skillet, heat 1 tablespoon of avocado oil over medium heat. Place the marinated tempeh in a single layer in the skillet. (You may need to cook it in batches.) Cook for 5 to 7 minutes, letting it brown before flipping over. Continue to cook on the other side for 3 to 5 minutes until browned and crispy.

4. Remove the tempeh and set aside. Add the remaining 1 tablespoon of avocado oil to the skillet. Add the rice and stir to distribute the oil.

CONTINUED

5. Push the rice to one side and add the egg to the other side of the skillet. Raise the heat to high and scramble the egg into the rice.

6. Add the broccoli, corn, and peas and cook for 2 to 3 minutes if fresh (5 to 6 minutes if frozen) until the veggies are brightly colored and just begin to soften. Add the remaining ¼ cup of soy sauce and the garlic and ginger, and cook for another minute.

7. Return the tempeh to the pan and toss with the rice and vegetables for 2 minutes or until the tempeh is heated through.

DAIRY-FREE • NUT-FREE • VEGAN

Per serving: Calories: 619; Fat: 18g; Carbs: 89g; Fiber: 6g; Sugar: 10g; Protein: 32g; Sodium: 989mg

Rice Noodles and Tofu with Peanut Sauce

SERVES 4

EQUIPMENT: Large nonstick skillet

PREP TIME: 45 minutes, plus 3 hours to press and marinate

COOK TIME: 20 minutes

The tofu takes a little preparation for this recipe, but once it's ready, the dish comes together quickly. Do not skip pressing the tofu, or the whole dish will be soggy. If you plan ahead, you can press the tofu overnight in the refrigerator. For a less time-consuming version, you can swap the tofu for 2 cups of frozen shelled edamame, and simply cook the edamame with the other vegetables.

1 (14-ounce) block extra-firm tofu

¼ cup low-sodium soy sauce

1 tablespoon sesame oil

1 tablespoon rice vinegar

½ teaspoon minced garlic

1½ tablespoons avocado oil or grapeseed oil, divided

8 ounces rice noodles

2 cups broccoli florets

1 cup shredded carrots

½ cup Spicy Peanut Sauce (page 21)

1. Place the tofu on a stack of paper towels, cover with additional paper towels, and set a heavy pan on top of it to squeeze out the extra moisture. Press the tofu for at least 2 hours.

2. After the tofu has been pressed, slice the block into quarters, and slice each quarter into ¼-inch-thick rectangles.

3. In a medium bowl, whisk together the soy sauce, sesame oil, vinegar, and garlic. Add the tofu and cover with plastic wrap. Marinate the tofu for at least 1 hour, but preferably overnight, in the refrigerator.

4. Soak the rice noodles in warm water according to the package directions, typically 20 to 30 minutes, then drain.

CONTINUED

5. In the meantime, in a large nonstick skillet, heat 1 tablespoon of avocado oil over medium heat until the oil is shimmering. Add the tofu, being careful not to crowd the pan. (You may need to cook it in batches.) Cook the tofu for 3 to 4 minutes until browned. Flip the pieces and continue to cook another 2 to 3 minutes until they are brown on both sides. Transfer to a paper towel to drain.

6. Add the remaining ½ tablespoon of avocado oil to the skillet and warm over medium heat. Add the broccoli and carrots. Cook for 5 to 6 minutes over medium-high heat until tender but still crisp.

7. Add the Spicy Peanut Sauce, rice noodles, and tofu, and continue to cook for 2 to 3 minutes until heated through. Be sure not to overcook or the noodles will turn soft and gummy.

Flexitarian tip: Swap the tofu for ½ pound of cooked shrimp—simply add them with the vegetables in step 6.

DAIRY-FREE • VEGAN

Per serving: Calories: 428; Fat: 16g; Carbs: 61g; Fiber: 3g; Sugar: 4g; Protein: 10g; Sodium: 732mg

Vegetable Pad Thai

Pad Thai is traditionally made with fish sauce, which isn't vegetarian, so this recipe substitutes soy sauce and tomato paste. This dish cooks quickly, so it helps to have all your ingredients chopped and ready before you begin. I like to prepare the vegetables while the rice noodles are soaking.

8 ounces rice noodles

2 tablespoons soy sauce

2 teaspoons tomato paste

2 teaspoons honey

3 teaspoons avocado oil or grapeseed oil, divided

1 cup shredded carrots

1 cup shredded purple cabbage

1 red bell pepper, seeded and cut into matchsticks

1 green bell pepper, seeded and cut into matchsticks

2 eggs

2 tablespoons crushed peanuts

½ cup chopped fresh cilantro

1. Soak the rice noodles in warm water according to the package directions, typically 20 to 30 minutes, then drain.

2. In the meantime, whisk together the soy sauce, tomato paste, and honey in a small bowl.

3. In a large nonstick skillet, heat 2 teaspoons of avocado oil over medium heat. Add the carrots, cabbage, and bell peppers and cook for 4 to 5 minutes. Remove the vegetables and set aside.

4. Add the remaining 1 teaspoon of oil to the skillet, then add the rice noodles and soy sauce mixture. Cook for 1 to 2 minutes over medium heat, then push to one side and add the eggs. Scramble the eggs for 1 to 2 minutes until set.

5. Add the cooked vegetables and stir everything together until evenly coated with sauce.

6. Remove from the heat and divide among 4 plates. Top with the peanuts and cilantro.

DAIRY-FREE
VEGAN: *Omit the eggs, and use agave nectar instead of honey.*

Per serving: Calories: 403; Fat: 13g; Carbs: 63g; Fiber: 5g; Sugar: 9g; Protein: 10g; Sodium: 738mg

Butternut Squash Macaroni and Cheese

SERVES 4
EQUIPMENT: Medium pot, large skillet, blender or food processor
PREP TIME: 15 minutes
COOK TIME: 15 minutes

The butternut squash in this recipe creates a thick and creamy sauce without the need for a lot of cheese. If you love macaroni and cheese but want a slightly lighter version, give this one a try! You can skip the sage if you don't have it, but it does add a lovely, subtle flavor to the sauce.

4 cups water

2 cups peeled and cubed butternut squash (about 1 pound)

2 tablespoons butter

10 fresh sage leaves

2 tablespoons whole-wheat flour

1 cup whole milk

⅓ cup shredded Parmesan cheese

8 ounces 100 percent whole-wheat macaroni

1. In a medium pot, bring the water to a boil. Add the butternut squash and boil for 7 to 9 minutes until soft enough to pierce with a fork.

2. While the squash is cooking, melt the butter in a large skillet over low heat. Add the sage and gently cook for 3 minutes to infuse the butter. Discard the sage leaves.

3. Raise the heat to medium. Whisk the flour into the butter and cook for 1 minute, stirring constantly. Whisk in the milk and continue to stir and simmer for 2 minutes until there are no lumps. Remove from the heat.

4. Drain the butternut squash and add to the skillet. Using a potato masher, mash the squash and the sauce to combine. Stir in the Parmesan cheese.

5. Let the mixture cool slightly, then carefully transfer to a blender or food processor and blend until smooth. If your blender has a cover with a removable insert in the center, remove the insert to allow steam to escape.

6. Cook the macaroni according to the package directions, then drain. Reserve a cup of the cooking water.

7. In a large bowl, combine the macaroni and squash sauce. If the sauce is too thick, stir in ¼ to ½ cup of reserved cooking water. Serve immediately.

NUT-FREE • SOY-FREE

DAIRY-FREE/VEGAN: *Use vegan butter or soy milk instead of whole milk, and ⅓ cup nutritional yeast instead of Parmesan. Add salt to taste.*

Per serving: Calories: 415; Fat: 11g; Carbs: 68g; Fiber: 7g; Sugar: 5g; Protein: 17g; Sodium: 171mg

Creamy Hummus Pasta

SERVES 4
EQUIPMENT: Large pot, blender or food processor
PREP TIME: 20 minutes
COOK TIME: 15 minutes

This recipe might sound a little strange, but you'll be pleasantly surprised how hummus can be the perfect base for a creamy sauce. The hummus adds a bit more protein and fiber to this meal, and served on top of whole-wheat pasta, you have a perfectly satisfying dish. This one reheats well for leftovers the next day, so I love making a double batch.

8 ounces 100 percent whole-wheat rotini

¾ cup canned chickpeas, drained and rinsed

2 garlic cloves

2 tablespoons olive oil

2 tablespoons tahini

2 teaspoons freshly squeezed lemon juice

½ teaspoon salt

2 tablespoons water

½ cup marinara sauce

Substitution tip: To save time, you can use store-bought garlic hummus rather than making your own. (Although this hummus is super easy to make!)

1. Bring a large pot of water to a boil. Add the rotini and cook according to the package directions, then drain. Reserve a cup of the cooking water.

2. While the pasta cooks, make the hummus: Place the chickpeas in a small microwave-safe bowl and microwave for 30 seconds. In a blender or food processor, process the warm chickpeas, garlic, olive oil, tahini, lemon juice, salt, and water for 2 minutes or until smooth.

3. In a large microwave-safe bowl, combine the hummus with the marinara sauce. Heat the mixture in the microwave for 30 seconds or until heated through. Or you can heat the sauce in a saucepan on the stove over medium heat for 2 to 3 minutes until heated through. If you'd like to thin the sauce, add a little of the pasta cooking water.

4. Combine the rotini with the sauce and serve immediately.

DAIRY-FREE • NUT-FREE • SOY-FREE • VEGAN

Per serving: Calories: 306; Fat: 13g; Carbs: 39g; Fiber: 6g; Sugar: 4g; Protein: 53g; Sodium: 434mg

Pasta Primavera

SERVES 4
EQUIPMENT: Large pot, large skillet
PREP TIME: 15 minutes
COOK TIME: 15 minutes

Need an easy, healthy, and colorful dinner idea? Look no further. This dish cooks up quickly and the rainbow of vegetables makes it deliciously filling and nutritious. If you don't have bell pepper or broccoli on hand, you can swap in any vegetables, such as shredded carrots or fresh peas, without missing a beat.

10 ounces 100 percent whole-wheat rotini

2 cups broccoli, cut into 1-inch pieces

1 red bell pepper, seeded and cut into thin strips

2 tablespoons olive oil (plus more for serving, if desired)

4 garlic cloves, thinly sliced

½ teaspoon red pepper flakes

2 cups cherry tomatoes, halved

½ teaspoon salt

¼ cup grated Parmesan cheese (optional)

Several fresh basil leaves, cut into ribbons (optional)

1. Bring a large pot of water to a boil. Add the rotini and begin cooking according to the package directions. When there are 2 minutes of cooking time left, add the broccoli and bell pepper to the pot. Drain, reserving a cup of the cooking water.

2. In a large skillet, heat the olive oil, garlic, and red pepper flakes over medium heat for 1 minute. Add the tomatoes, salt, and 1 tablespoon of the cooking water, and continue to cook for 3 minutes or until the tomatoes begin to wilt slightly.

3. Add the rotini and vegetables to the skillet. Stir until the pasta is completely coated.

4. To serve, drizzle with more olive oil, season with salt, and top with Parmesan cheese and basil (if using).

Substitution tip: I love using chickpea noodles for this dish, which are made from chickpea flour. They have more protein and fiber than regular pasta, making them extra filling. That would also make the dish gluten-free.

NUT-FREE • SOY-FREE
DAIRY-FREE/VEGAN: *Skip the cheese.*

Per serving: Calories: 319; Fat: 9g; Carbs: 55g; Fiber: 9g; Sugar: 5g; Protein: 10g; Sodium: 322mg

Creamy Asparagus and Goat Cheese Pasta

SERVES 4
EQUIPMENT: Large pot
PREP TIME: 10 minutes
COOK TIME: 20 minutes

This dish is super easy to make but tastes like you spent hours cooking the sauce, and only one pot to clean up! This recipe calls for whole-wheat noodles, but I often make it with chickpea pasta—which is gluten-free.

1 pound asparagus, ends trimmed

12 ounces 100 percent whole-wheat rotini

6 ounces goat cheese, at room temperature

¼ teaspoon garlic powder

¼ teaspoon salt

Pinch red pepper flakes

1. Fill a large bowl with ice water.

2. Bring a large pot of water to a boil. Cook the asparagus for 2 to 4 minutes, depending on the thickness, until bright green and tender. Remove from the pot (reserving the water) and submerge in the ice bath.

3. Bring the water back to a boil. Cook the rotini according to the package directions. Drain, reserving a cup of the cooking water, and return the rotini to the pot.

4. In a medium bowl, combine ¼ cup of the cooking water with the goat cheese, garlic powder, salt, and red pepper flakes.

5. Cut the asparagus into 1-inch pieces. Stir the asparagus and goat cheese sauce into the rotini. Heat over low heat for 1 minute, stirring until the sauce is heated through.

6. Serve with additional red pepper flakes, if desired.

NUT-FREE • SOY-FREE
DAIRY-FREE/VEGAN: *Use an equal amount of vegan ricotta for a creamy sauce.*
GLUTEN-FREE: *Use chickpea pasta.*

Per serving: Calories: 400; Fat: 10g; Carbs: 60g; Fiber: 10g; Sugar: 5g; Protein: 19g; Sodium: 318mg

Spinach and Mushroom Pasta

SERVES 4
EQUIPMENT: Large pot, large skillet
PREP TIME: 15 minutes
COOK TIME: 15 minutes

My husband loves mushrooms and I love pasta, so this meal is a happy compromise. Mushrooms have very few calories, but they add a lot of volume to this dish, which helps increase the serving size without adding carbohydrates. Feel free to season your meal with extra red pepper flakes or oregano. I love the additional spice.

8 ounces 100 percent whole-wheat spaghetti

1 teaspoon olive oil, plus 1 tablespoon

2 cups sliced mushrooms

Salt

Freshly ground black pepper

4 garlic cloves, minced

4 cups baby spinach

2 teaspoons freshly squeezed lemon juice

¼ teaspoon red pepper flakes

¼ teaspoon dried oregano

8 to 10 fresh basil leaves, cut into thin strips (about 2 tablespoons)

2 tablespoons pine nuts

¼ cup shredded Parmesan cheese

1. Bring a large pot of water to a boil. Cook the spaghetti according to the package directions, then drain.

2. In a large skillet, heat 1 teaspoon of olive oil over medium heat. Add the mushrooms and season with salt and pepper. Cook over medium heat for 12 minutes, stirring occasionally. Add the garlic and spinach and cook for 3 minutes more. Add the lemon juice.

3. Add the spaghetti and season with more salt and pepper. Add the red pepper flakes, oregano, and basil, and stir until combined.

4. Top with the remaining 1 tablespoon of olive oil, the pine nuts, and the Parmesan cheese just before serving.

SOY-FREE
DAIRY-FREE/VEGAN: *Skip the Parmesan and add an extra 2 tablespoons pine nuts.*

Per serving: Calories: 277; Fat: 10g; Carbs: 37g; Fiber: 6g; Sugar: 3g; Protein: 12g; Sodium: 425mg

Ingredient tip: I like to use a variety of mushrooms in this dish for lots of flavor. I typically go with porcini, cremini, and button varieties, but choose whatever you like.

Roasted Red Pepper Pasta

SERVES 4

EQUIPMENT: Baking sheet, large baking dish, large pot, blender or food processor
PREP TIME: 20 minutes
COOK TIME: 45 minutes

This pasta sauce requires just a few simple ingredients, but it's a delicious combination. I love the hint of sweetness from the peppers, and roasting them until they begin to blacken brings out a deep, rich flavor. Ten cloves of garlic might sound like a lot, but once it's roasted, the flavor mellows and becomes sweet.

4 red bell peppers

1 pound Roma tomatoes

10 garlic cloves, peeled

1 pound 100 percent whole-wheat angel-hair pasta

1 tablespoon olive oil

Salt

1. Preheat the oven to 400°F. Line a baking sheet with parchment paper.

2. Cut the bell peppers in half lengthwise and remove the seeds. Place the bell peppers cut-side down on the prepared baking sheet.

3. Cut the tomatoes in half. Place them and the garlic in a large baking dish.

4. Roast the bell peppers, tomatoes, and garlic for 10 to 15 minutes until the peppers have started to blacken.

5. Set the tomatoes aside to cool. Using tongs, carefully transfer the bell peppers to a large bowl, cover with aluminum foil, and let sit for 15 minutes.

132

The Truly Healthy Vegetarian Cookbook

6. In the meantime, bring a large pot of water to a boil. Add the pasta and cook according to the package directions, then drain.

7. When they are cool enough to handle, peel the skin off the peppers and tomatoes. The skin should slide off, or use your hands to pull it off.

8. Place the peeled peppers, peeled tomatoes, garlic, and olive oil in a blender or food processor. Blend until smooth. Season with salt.

9. Top the pasta with the red pepper sauce and serve immediately.

Ingredient tip: Red peppers are a great source of vitamin C, vitamin B$_6$, and antioxidants.

DAIRY-FREE • NUT-FREE • SOY-FREE • VEGAN
GLUTEN-FREE: *Use chickpea pasta.*

Per serving: Calories: 276; Fat: 5g; Carbs: 53g; Fiber: 9g; Sugar: 9g; Protein: 10g; Sodium: 86mg

Vegetable Lasagna

SERVES 4

EQUIPMENT: 8-by-8-inch baking dish
PREP TIME: 25 minutes
COOK TIME: 35 minutes

When I was a child, my mom would often make lasagna when we had company over, so it always feels special to me. As much as I love the cheese and noodles, I like sneaking in extra vegetables to make the serving size a little bigger and give the dish a nutritional boost. Make sure you buy whole-wheat lasagna noodles, as they have a lot more protein and fiber than regular noodles. Sizes may vary, but look for noodles that are close to 7½ inches by 3½ inches, which are easy to layer in an 8-by-8-inch baking dish.

1 pound zucchini

2 cups marinara sauce

8 100 percent whole-wheat no-boil lasagna noodles (7½ inches by 3½ inches)

1½ cups baby spinach

1½ cups whole-milk ricotta cheese

¾ cup shredded mozzarella cheese

1. Preheat the oven to 375°F.

2. Using a vegetable peeler, slice the zucchini into long, flat ribbons, until you hit the seedy part. Discard the seedy part, or save for another use. (The seedy ribbons will make the lasagna watery.)

3. Spread a thin layer of marinara sauce on the bottom of an 8-by-8-inch baking dish.

4. Place 2 lasagna noodles at the bottom of the pan to form the first layer. Add a layer of zucchini ribbons. Layer on ½ cup of spinach. Spoon ½ cup of ricotta on top of the spinach, then add ½ cup marinara sauce.

5. Continue to layer noodles, zucchini, spinach, ricotta, and sauce twice more. Add one more layer of noodles and sauce. Top with the mozzarella.

6. Cover with aluminum foil and bake for 25 minutes. Remove the foil and continue to bake for 10 minutes or until the cheese is bubbly.

7. Let the lasagna stand for 5 minutes before serving, so that it will be set and less watery.

NUT-FREE • SOY-FREE
DAIRY-FREE/VEGAN: *Use vegan ricotta for the filling and soy mozzarella on top.*

Per serving: Calories: 426; Fat: 9g; Carbs: 66g; Fiber: 11g; Sugar: 14g; Protein: 21g; Sodium: 646mg

Chocolate Trail Mix Bark, page 141

CHAPTER 10

Desserts

Eating healthy food doesn't mean skipping dessert! The recipes in this chapter will satisfy your sweet tooth but keep things clean by using just a bit of unrefined sugar and whole-wheat flours. You'll also notice a few recipes that use beans. (Don't worry, no one will be able to tell!) These recipes contain small amounts of sweetener with plenty of other healthy ingredients. Whether you need a little after-dinner treat or you're looking for something sweet to bring to a party, you'll find your new favorite desserts right here.

Frozen Yogurt Bites

MAKES 8 BITES [2 BITES = 1 SERVING]
EQUIPMENT: 8- or 12-cup muffin pan
PREP TIME: 10 minutes, plus 3 hours to freeze

These frozen yogurt bites make a great summer treat. I like to use wild blueberries because they're smaller and easier to mix into each bite, but you can use regular frozen or fresh blueberries if you like. The granola topping gives these a nice crunch and an extra dose of protein and fiber.

¾ cup plain Greek yogurt

1½ teaspoons honey

½ cup frozen wild blueberries

2 tablespoons Grain-Free Granola (page 33)

1. Line 8 cups of a muffin pan with paper or silicone liners.

2. In a small bowl, mix the yogurt and honey. Gently stir in the blueberries.

3. Scoop 2 tablespoons of the yogurt mixture into each of 8 muffin cups.

4. Sprinkle the top of each cup with Grain-Free Granola.

5. Freeze for at least 3 hours until set.

Substitution tip: You can use any frozen or fresh fruit for these bites; just chop it up into small pieces before adding to the yogurt. Fresh strawberries work especially well.

GLUTEN-FREE • LOW-CARB • SOY-FREE
DAIRY-FREE: *Use almond milk yogurt or coconut milk yogurt.*
VEGAN: *Use agave nectar instead of honey.*

Per serving: Calories: 70; Fat: 0g; Carbs: 12g; Fiber: 0g; Sugar: 10g; Protein: 4g; Sodium: 20mg

Chocolate-Banana Nice Cream

SERVES 4

EQUIPMENT: High-powered blender (like a Vitamix) or food processor
PREP TIME: 15 minutes

It's hard to believe that with just a few ingredients, you can make soft serve-style ice cream at home without all the saturated fat and added sugar. If you don't have a high-powered blender or a food processor, you can still make this! Just be sure to cut the bananas into very small pieces before freezing (see Prep tip), and you might need to add an extra tablespoon of almond milk to help it blend.

3 cups frozen banana chunks (from about 4 large very ripe bananas)

2 tablespoons unsweetened cocoa powder

1 to 2 tablespoons almond milk

Pinch salt

1 to 2 teaspoons honey (optional)

1. In a high-powered blender or food processor, begin to blend the frozen banana chunks and cocoa powder.

2. Add the almond milk and continue to blend to create a smooth consistency. Add the salt and blend until smooth.

3. Taste and see if you need to add honey. If your bananas were very ripe, the ice cream is probably sweet enough, but if not, blend in a bit of honey.

4. Serve immediately, or freeze for 10 to 15 minutes if desired. If you freeze it longer, it'll harden.

Prep tip: Slice ripe bananas and place the slices on a baking sheet in the freezer. Once frozen, transfer them to a freezer bag until you're ready to use them. The slices will be easier to process than whole frozen bananas.

DAIRY-FREE • GLUTEN-FREE • LOW-CARB • SOY-FREE
VEGAN: *Use maple syrup instead of honey.*

Per serving: Calories: 111; Fat: 1g; Carbs: 28g; Fiber: 4g; Sugar: 15g; Protein: 2g; Sodium: 41mg

Lemon Pie Bites

MAKES 8 BITES [1 BITE = 1 SERVING]
EQUIPMENT: Blender or food processor
PREP TIME: 15 minutes

These lemon pie bites are naturally sweetened with dates, and since they're loaded with nuts, they have a good balance of healthy fat and protein. These are a perfect sweet treat when you need an afternoon pick-me-up.

½ cup cashews

½ cup almonds

½ cup dates

1 tablespoon freshly squeezed lemon juice

¾ teaspoon pure vanilla extract

Almond flour or unsweetened shredded coconut, for rolling (optional)

1. Put the cashews, almonds, and dates in a blender or food processor and blend for 30 seconds.

2. Add the lemon juice and vanilla, and continue to blend until incorporated. You may need to scrape down the sides with a rubber spatula.

3. Carefully transfer the mixture to a piece of parchment paper. Separate the mixture into rounded tablespoons and roll into 1-inch balls.

4. If they're sticky, you can roll them in almond flour or shredded coconut.

5. Store the bites in an airtight container in the refrigerator for up to 1 week.

DAIRY-FREE • GLUTEN-FREE • LOW-CARB
SOY-FREE • VEGAN

Per bite: Calories: 116; Fat: 7g; Carbs: 13g; Fiber: 2g; Sugar: 8g; Protein: 3g; Sodium: 2mg

Chocolate Trail Mix Bark

SERVES 6
EQUIPMENT: Baking sheet
PREP TIME: 10 minutes, plus 30 minutes to chill
COOK TIME: 5 minutes

This is one of my favorite last-minute desserts to throw together when we have friends over. The sweet-and-salty combination keeps people coming back for more. To keep this dessert vegan and dairy-free, be sure to use vegan dark chocolate chips. Look for ones that are at least 70 percent cacao, which has less added sugar than milk chocolate or semisweet chocolate. Cacao is also a good source of iron. Store this bark in the refrigerator, as the chocolate will start to melt if it's left out for too long.

1 cup vegan dark chocolate chips

1 tablespoon shredded coconut

1 tablespoon dried cranberries

1 tablespoon pumpkin seeds

1 tablespoon walnuts, broken into pieces

1 tablespoon pecans, broken into pieces

Pinch coarse sea salt

Substitution tip: You can easily swap in other dried fruits and nuts of your choice. Try dried cherries and cashew pieces.

1. Line a baking sheet with wax paper or parchment paper.

2. Melt the chocolate chips in a microwave-safe bowl by heating in the microwave on 50 percent power, stirring every 30 seconds until smooth. Or melt them in a small saucepan over low heat, stirring frequently with a wooden spoon.

3. Pour the melted chocolate onto the prepared baking sheet and spread into a thin, even layer using the back of a spoon or a rubber spatula.

4. Sprinkle with the coconut, cranberries, pumpkin seeds, walnuts, pecans, and sea salt. Gently press the toppings into the chocolate and chill in the refrigerator for 30 minutes.

5. Break into bite-size pieces and store in the refrigerator.

DAIRY-FREE • GLUTEN-FREE • LOW-CARB
SOY-FREE • VEGAN

Per serving: Calories: 120; Fat: 8g; Carbs: 14g; Fiber: 0g; Sugar: 11g; Protein: 2g; Sodium: 40mg

Baked Stuffed Apples

EQUIPMENT: 8-by-8-inch baking dish
PREP TIME: 15 minutes
COOK TIME: 55 minutes

These are such a delicious treat to make in the fall when apples are in season. I like to use crunchy red apples like Braeburn, Gala, or Fuji. Look for apples that are about the size of a tennis ball. You don't want them to be too big, but you need enough room for the filling.

½ cup gluten-free rolled oats

½ cup chopped walnuts

¼ cup unsweetened dried cranberries

1 teaspoon ground cinnamon

1 teaspoon pure vanilla extract

Pinch salt

1 tablespoon coconut oil

4 medium red apples

1. Preheat the oven to 350°F.

2. In a large mixing bowl, combine the oats, walnuts, cranberries, cinnamon, vanilla, salt, and coconut oil. It may be easiest to mix with a fork or your fingers.

3. Using a sharp paring knife, carefully core the apples: Insert the blade into the top of the apple, just outside of the core, about 1½ inches deep. Carefully remove the blade and continue to cut a square pattern around the core of the apple, without cutting all the way to the bottom. Use a spoon to gently scoop out the core.

4. Spoon the filling into each apple.

5. Place the apples in an 8-by-8-inch baking dish and add a very shallow layer of water to the bottom of the dish, about ½ cup.

6. Cover with aluminum foil and bake for 45 to 55 minutes until the apples are tender when pierced with a fork.

DAIRY-FREE • GLUTEN-FREE • SOY-FREE • VEGAN

Per serving: Calories: 195; Fat: 7g; Carbs: 36g; Fiber: 7g; Sugar: 24g; Protein: 2g; Sodium: 41mg

142   The Truly Healthy Vegetarian Cookbook

Blueberry Crumble

This blueberry crumble takes only a few minutes to assemble, so you can have it in the oven in no time. Frozen berries tend to be cheaper and more readily available, which means you can make this even when berries aren't in season. This crumble is also great with blackberries, although they may need a bit more honey to balance their tartness.

For the filling

Nonstick cooking spray

2 cups frozen blueberries, thawed

2 tablespoons whole-wheat flour

2 tablespoons honey

For the crumble

½ cup rolled oats

¼ cup unrefined coconut sugar

¼ cup whole-wheat flour

¼ cup coconut oil

Pinch cinnamon

Pinch salt

Ingredient tip: If you don't have coconut sugar, you can substitute brown sugar—but coconut sugar is a less refined sweetener.

TO MAKE THE FILLING

1. Preheat the oven to 425°F. Spray an 8-by-8-inch baking dish with nonstick cooking spray.

2. In a medium bowl, gently stir the blueberries with the flour until the juice from the berries has thickened. Drizzle with the honey and gently stir. Spread the blueberry mixture into the prepared baking dish.

TO MAKE THE CRUMBLE

1. In a medium bowl, combine the oats, coconut sugar, and flour. Use a fork to press the coconut oil into the oat mixture, until crumbly.

2. Top the blueberries with the oat mixture. Sprinkle with the cinnamon and salt.

3. Bake for 30 to 40 minutes until the top is browned.

4. Let sit for 5 to 7 minutes before serving.

DAIRY-FREE • NUT-FREE • SOY-FREE

VEGAN: *Substitute agave nectar or maple syrup for the honey.*

Per serving: Calories: 292; Fat: 15g; Carbs: 42g; Fiber: 3g; Sugar: 29g; Protein: 2g; Sodium: 40mg

Chocolate-Avocado Cookies

MAKES 12 COOKIES [1 COOKIE = 1 SERVING]
EQUIPMENT: Food processor or blender, nonstick baking sheet
PREP TIME: 15 minutes
COOK TIME: 10 minutes

These cookies don't require any butter or oil, thanks to the creamy avocado. Just be sure to blend the batter well before adding the flour. It can be hard to tell when these cookies are baked, since they won't turn brown, so be careful not to overbake. I recommend checking after 8 minutes.

1 avocado

1 large egg

1 teaspoon pure vanilla extract

½ cup unrefined coconut sugar

¼ teaspoon salt

1 teaspoon baking soda

½ cup whole-wheat pastry flour

½ cup unsweetened cocoa powder

¼ cup dark chocolate chips

1. Preheat the oven to 350°F.

2. In a food processor or blender, combine the avocado, egg, vanilla, and coconut sugar. Blend until completely smooth.

3. Transfer the avocado mixture to a large mixing bowl and stir in the salt, baking soda, flour, and cocoa. Add the dark chocolate chips and mix to distribute.

4. Drop rounded tablespoons of the cookie dough onto a nonstick baking sheet.

5. Bake for 8 to 9 minutes. *Do not* overbake!

6. Let the cookies cool for a few minutes before removing from the pan.

Ingredient tip: Unrefined coconut sugar is less processed than regular sugar, but it's still sugar and should be eaten in moderation. If you don't have coconut sugar, you can replace it with brown sugar.

LOW-CARB • NUT-FREE • SOY-FREE
DAIRY-FREE: *High-quality dark chocolate chips tend to be dairy-free, but check the package to be sure.*

Per cookie: Calories: 111; Fat: 5g; Carbs: 17g; Fiber: 3g; Sugar: 10g; Protein: 2g; Sodium: 162mg

Chocolate Chip Chickpea Cookies

MAKES 12 COOKIES [1 COOKIE = 1 SERVING]
EQUIPMENT: Blender or food processor, nonstick baking sheet
PREP TIME: 15 minutes
COOK TIME: 15 minutes

I know, it sounds crazy, but I can promise you, not a single person will guess there are chickpeas in these cookies. It's a great way to add a bit of protein and fiber to your dessert, and the texture is incredible. If you love a soft-baked cookie, you must give these a try.

1 (15-ounce) can chickpeas, drained and rinsed

½ cup unsalted cashew butter

⅓ cup maple syrup

2 teaspoons pure vanilla extract

½ teaspoon baking soda

½ teaspoon baking powder

1 teaspoon salt

½ cup dark chocolate chips

Substitution tip: Cashew butter is my personal favorite, but if you don't have any, you can use peanut butter or almond butter instead.

1. Preheat the oven to 350°F.

2. Blend the chickpeas and cashew butter in a blender or food processor on high for 1 minute. Add the maple syrup and vanilla and blend for 2 to 3 minutes more, scraping down the sides after every minute. You want the mixture to be entirely free of lumps.

3. Add the baking soda, baking powder, and salt, then blend for 30 seconds.

4. If necessary, let the batter cool, then add the chocolate chips. (If the batter is too warm from blending, the chocolate will melt.)

5. Drop rounded tablespoons of the cookie dough onto a nonstick baking sheet. The cookies will spread out slightly, so be sure to leave a few inches of space between cookies.

6. Bake for 12 to 14 minutes until the cookies are brown on the edges.

GLUTEN-FREE • LOW-CARB • SOY-FREE
DAIRY-FREE/VEGAN: *High-quality dark chocolate chips tend to be dairy-free and vegan, but check the package to be sure.*

Per cookie: Calories: 216; Fat: 12g; Carbs: 24g; Fiber: 2g; Sugar: 9g; Protein: 5g; Sodium: 366mg

Maple Peanut Butter Cookies

MAKES 12 COOKIES [1 COOKIE = 1 SERVING]
EQUIPMENT: Baking sheet, blender or food processor
PREP TIME: 10 minutes
COOK TIME: 10 minutes

These gluten-free peanut butter cookies are so soft, they practically melt in your mouth. You can also make these with almond butter for a slightly different flavor. Be sure to use whole-grain rolled oats, not instant oatmeal.

1 cup gluten-free whole-grain rolled oats

1 cup salted creamy peanut butter

⅔ cup maple syrup

2 teaspoons vanilla extract

1 teaspoon baking soda

⅛ teaspoon fine salt

1. Preheat the oven to 350°F. Line a baking sheet with parchment paper.

2. Blend the oats in a blender or food processor until they're a chunky flour texture.

3. In a large bowl, mix the peanut butter, maple syrup, and vanilla until well combined.

4. In a medium bowl, combine the oats, baking soda, and salt. Add the oat mixture to the peanut butter mixture.

5. Drop rounded tablespoons of the cookie dough onto the prepared baking sheet.

6. Bake for 9 to 12 minutes until lightly browned on the edges.

7. Let the cookies cool completely before removing them from the baking sheet. They'll be fragile when you first remove them from the oven.

Prep tip: Be careful, because these cookies tend to brown on the bottom. Depending on your oven, you might want to move them up to the top rack for the last few minutes of baking.

DAIRY-FREE • GLUTEN-FREE • LOW-CARB
SOY-FREE • VEGAN

Per cookie: Calories: 187; Fat: 11g; Carbs: 18g; Fiber: 2g; Sugar: 13g; Protein: 6g; Sodium: 228mg

Vegan Black Bean Brownie Bites

MAKES 16 TO 18 BROWNIES [1 BROWNIE = 1 SERVING]

EQUIPMENT: Blender or food processor, mini muffin pan

PREP TIME: 10 minutes

COOK TIME: 20 minutes

These flourless brownies get their fudgy texture from black beans, but no one will be able to tell. Be sure to blend the batter until it's completely smooth before stirring in the chocolate chips. That's essential to achieving the perfect black bean brownie bite!

1 (15-ounce) can black beans, drained and rinsed

½ cup honey

½ cup unsweetened Dutch cocoa powder

2 tablespoons coconut oil, melted

1 teaspoon pure vanilla extract

1 teaspoon baking powder

½ cup dark chocolate chips

Nonstick cooking spray

Ingredient tip: Dutch cocoa has a smoother, more mellow flavor compared to regular cocoa powder, but feel free to substitute regular cocoa powder if that's what you have in your pantry.

1. Preheat the oven to 350°F.

2. Combine the black beans, honey, cocoa, coconut oil, vanilla, and baking powder in a blender or food processor. Blend on high for 4 to 5 minutes, scraping the sides down after every minute, until the batter is mostly smooth.

3. If the batter is warm from blending, let it cool, then stir in the chocolate chips.

4. Spray a mini muffin pan with nonstick cooking spray. Scoop 1½ tablespoons of batter into each muffin cup.

5. Bake for 20 minutes or until the brownies begin to pull away from the sides of the pan just slightly. Do not overbake!

6. Let the brownies cool completely before removing them from the pan.

7. Store in an airtight container.

GLUTEN-FREE • LOW-CARB • NUT-FREE • SOY-FREE DAIRY-FREE/VEGAN: *High-quality dark chocolate chips tend to be dairy-free and vegan, but check the package.*

Per bite: Calories: 85; Fat: 3g; Carbs: 15g; Fiber: 2g; Sugar: 11g; Protein: 2g; Sodium: 2mg

PREP AND COOK VEGETABLE CHART

Vegetable	How to prepare it	Cooking method	Best way to eat
ASPARAGUS	Trim ends	Blanched, roasted, sautéed	Salads, pasta dishes
BELL PEPPERS	Remove stem and seeds	Raw, roasted, baked	Sauces, soups, stuffed with vegetables
BRUSSELS SPROUTS	Trim bottoms	Sautéed, roasted, broiled, raw	Salads
BUTTERNUT SQUASH	Peel, remove seeds	Roasted, boiled, puréed	Salads, soups, sauces
CARROTS	Peel	Raw, boiled, roasted	Salads, soups
CAULIFLOWER	Remove outer leaves	Broiled, roasted, riced, steamed	Soups and stews, stir-fries, tacos
EDAMAME	Shell or keep in pods	Steamed, boiled	Stir-fries, salads
EGGPLANT	Remove stem	Roasted, broiled, simmered	Soups and stews, stuffed with vegetables
GREEN BEANS	Trim ends	Blanched, roasted, sautéed, stir-fried	Salads, stir-fries
KALE	Remove stems, massage leaves	Raw, sautéed	Salads, soups
SWEET POTATO	Scrub skin	Roasted	Fries, salads
ZUCCHINI	Trim ends	Shaved into noodles, sautéed, roasted	Substitute for pasta, soups and stews, fries

PRODUCE STORAGE GUIDE

There's nothing worse than produce that spoils before you can eat it. Here are my favorite tips and tricks for keeping your vegetables fresh as long as possible:

- Most delicate herbs, like parsley, cilantro, and dill, should be kept in the refrigerator and treated like fresh flowers. Trim the ends of the stems and place the herbs upright in a glass jar with an inch of water in the bottom. Gently cover with a plastic bag and seal with a rubber band. Basil should also be stored in a jar of water and loosely covered, but left at room temperature.

- For hardy herbs like sage, thyme, and rosemary, wash and then wrap them loosely in a paper towel, place in a plastic bag or wrap with plastic wrap, and store in the refrigerator.

- Asparagus stalks should be trimmed at the bottom and placed upright in a glass with 1 inch of water and stored in the refrigerator. They can be loosely covered with plastic. You may need to refresh the water after a day or two.

- Kale should be stored in an open plastic bag in the crisper drawer. If you prefer to wash it ahead of time, keep it in a sealed plastic bag with a paper towel inside to keep it dry.

- Unripened avocados can be left on the counter. To help them ripen more quickly, place in a paper bag. Once ripe, store in the refrigerator to slow the ripening process.

- Mushrooms should be kept in the refrigerator in a brown paper bag. Leave packaged mushrooms in the container and store them in the refrigerator.

- Brussels sprouts, if removed from the stalk, should be stored in the refrigerator in an open container with a damp towel placed on top.

- Zucchini, yellow squash, and bell peppers are best stored in a loose plastic bag in the refrigerator.

- Broccoli and cauliflower should be stored in an airtight bag or container in the refrigerator.

- Potatoes, winter squash, garlic, and onions should be stored in a cool, dry, dark place, such as in a bin in a corner of the pantry.

MEASUREMENT CONVERSIONS

VOLUME EQUIVALENTS (LIQUID)

US Standard	US Standard (ounces)	Metric (approximate)
2 tablespoons	1 fl. oz.	30 mL
¼ cup	2 fl. oz.	60 mL
½ cup	4 fl. oz.	120 mL
1 cup	8 fl. oz.	240 mL
1½ cups	12 fl. oz.	355 mL
2 cups or 1 pint	16 fl. oz.	475 mL
4 cups or 1 quart	32 fl. oz.	1 L
1 gallon	128 fl. oz.	4 L

OVEN TEMPERATURES

Fahrenheit (F)	Celsius (C) (approximate)
250°F	120°C
300°F	150°C
325°F	165°C
350°F	180°C
375°F	190°C
400°F	200°C
425°F	220°C
450°F	230°C

VOLUME EQUIVALENTS (DRY)

US Standard	Metric (approximate)
⅛ teaspoon	0.5 mL
¼ teaspoon	1 mL
½ teaspoon	2 mL
¾ teaspoon	4 mL
1 teaspoon	5 mL
1 tablespoon	15 mL
¼ cup	59 mL
⅓ cup	79 mL
½ cup	118 mL
⅔ cup	156 mL
¾ cup	177 mL
1 cup	235 mL
2 cups or 1 pint	475 mL
3 cups	700 mL
4 cups or 1 quart	1 L

WEIGHT EQUIVALENTS

US Standard	Metric (approximate)
½ ounce	15 g
1 ounce	30 g
2 ounces	60 g
4 ounces	115 g
8 ounces	225 g
12 ounces	340 g
16 ounces or 1 pound	455 g

THE DIRTY DOZEN
& THE CLEAN FIFTEEN™

The Environmental Working Group (EWG) is a nonprofit, nonpartisan organization dedicated to protecting human health and the environment. Its mission is to empower people to live healthier lives in a healthier environment. This organization publishes an annual list of the twelve kinds of produce, in sequence, that have the highest amount of pesticide residue—the Dirty Dozen—as well as a list of the fifteen kinds of produce that have the least amount of pesticide residue—the Clean Fifteen.

THE DIRTY DOZEN

The 2017 Dirty Dozen includes the following produce. These are considered among the year's most important produce to buy organic:

Strawberries	Grapes
Apples	Cherries
Nectarines	Spinach
Pears	Tomatoes
Peaches	Bell peppers
Potatoes	Kale/collard greens*
Celery	Hot peppers*

The Dirty Dozen list contains two additional items—kale/collard greens and hot peppers—because they tend to contain trace levels of highly hazardous pesticides.

THE CLEAN FIFTEEN

The least critical to buy organically are the Clean Fifteen list. The following are on the 2017 list:

Avocados	Papayas
Corn**	Kiwi
Pineapples	Eggplant
Cabbage	Honeydew
Sweet peas	Grapefruit
Onions	Cantaloupe
Asparagus	Cauliflower
Mangos	

*** Some of the sweet corn sold in the United States is grown from genetically engineered (GE) seedstock. Buy organic varieties of these crops to avoid GE produce.*

REFERENCES

Down to Earth. "Top 10 Reasons Why It's Green to Go Veggie." Accessed January 5, 2018. https://www.downtoearth.org/go-veggie/environment/top-10-reasons.

Flynn, Mary M., and Andrew R. Schiff. "Economical Healthy Diets (2012): Including Lean Animal Protein Costs More Than Using Extra Virgin Olive Oil." *Journal of Hunger & Environmental Nutrition* 10, no. 4 (September 2015): 467–82. doi:10.1080/19320248.2015.1045675.

Food and Agriculture Organization of the United Nations. "Livestock a Major Threat to the Environment." Updated November 29, 2006. http://www.fao.org/newsroom/en/news/2006/1000448/index.html.

Institute of Medicine. *Dietary Reference Intakes for Vitamin A, Vitamin K, Arsenic, Boron, Chromium, Copper, Iodine, Iron, Manganese, Molybdenum, Nickel, Silicon, Vanadium, and Zinc.* Washington, DC: National Academies Press, 2001.

Lynch, Sean R., and James D. Cook. "Interaction of Vitamin C and Iron." *Annals of the New York Academy of Sciences* no. 355 (1980): 32–44. https://www.ncbi.nlm.nih.gov/pubmed/6940487.

Pettersen, B. J., R. Anousheh, J. Fan, K. Jaceldo-Siegl, and G. E. Fraser. "Vegetarian Diets and Blood Pressure among White Subjects: Results from the Adventist Health Study-2 (AHS-2)." *Public Health Nutrition* 15, no. 10 (October 2012): 1901–16. doi:10.1017/S1368980011003454.

Rizzo, Nico S., Karen Jaceldo-Siegl, Joan Sabate, and Gary E. Fraser. "Nutrient Profiles of Vegetarian and Nonvegetarian Dietary Patterns." *Journal of the Academy of Nutrition and Dietetics* 113, no. 12 (December 2013): 1610–19. doi:10.1016/j.jand.2013.06.349.

Tonstad, Serena, Terry Butler, Ru Yan, and Gary E. Fraser. "Type of Vegetarian Diet, Body Weight, and Prevalence of Type 2 Diabetes." *Diabetes Care* 32, no. 5 (May 2009): 791–96. doi:10.2337/dc08-1886.

RECIPE INDEX

INDEX

ACKNOWLEDGMENTS

To the wonderful editorial staff and design team at Rockridge Press, thank you for making this dream a reality.

To my incredibly patient and wonderful parents who have supported me, believed in me, and encouraged me every step of the way.

To my grandma, who has been my fist-pumping cheerleader from the very start.

To Mark and Aricka, who are always willing to dream big, problem solve, and brainstorm with me.

To the Thomson family for their love and encouragement.

To Alexa, my voice of reason and unwavering support, who spent years telling me to write a book.

To Annie, for sending me daily encouragement, advice, and laughter, one snap at a time.

And to Alex, my chief taste tester, who gives me complete control of the kitchen. Thank you for giving me the confidence to face new challenges and pursue my passions.

ABOUT THE AUTHOR

ELIZABETH THOMSON is the foodie behind the vegetarian food blog *I Heart Vegetables*. She enjoys sharing simple, delicious recipes with her readers and coming up with new ways to help people live a healthier life. When she's not in the kitchen, she can be found exploring the restaurant scene in Richmond, Virginia.

CPSIA information can be obtained
at www.ICGtesting.com
Printed in the USA
BVOW11s2334290318
511496BV00001B/1/P